Outsiders Within

Outsiders Within

*Black Women in the Legal Academy
after Brown v. Board*

Elwood Watson

ROWMAN & LITTLEFIELD PUBLISHERS, INC.
Lanham • Boulder • New York • Toronto • Plymouth, UK

ROWMAN & LITTLEFIELD PUBLISHERS, INC.

Published in the United States of America
by Rowman & Littlefield Publishers, Inc.
A wholly owned subsidiary of The Rowman & Littlefield Publishing Group, Inc.
4501 Forbes Boulevard, Suite 200, Lanham, Maryland 20706
www.rowmanlittlefield.com

Estover Road
Plymouth PL6 7PY
United Kingdom

Copyright © 2008 by Rowman & Littlefield Publishers, Inc.
First paperback edition 2009

British Library Cataloguing in Publication Information Available

Library of Congress Cataloging-in-Publication Data:

Watson, Elwood.
  Outsiders within : black women in the legal academy after Brown v. Board / Elwood
Watson.
      p. cm.
  1. African American women lawyers. 2. African Americans—Legal status, laws, etc.
I. Title.
  KF299.A35W38 2008
  340.082—dc22   2007050243

  ISBN: 978-0-7425-4073-6 (cloth : alk. paper)
  ISBN: 978-0-7425-4074-3 (pbk. : alk. paper)
  ISBN: 978-0-7425-9980-2 (electronic)

Printed in the United States of America

♾™ The paper used in this publication meets the minimum requirements of
American National Standard for Information Sciences—Permanence of Paper
for Printed Library Materials, ANSI/NISO Z39.48-1992.

~

Contents

Acknowledgments   vii

Introduction   1

Chapter 1   In the Media Spotlight: Anita Hill and Lani Guinier   13

Chapter 2   A Hostile and Unsupportive Environment   49

Chapter 3   Dealing with the Multiple Isms: Racism, Sexism, Elitism   71

Chapter 4   Affirmative Action: Combating Assumptions   93

Chapter 5   Interacting with Students: That Delicate Balance   109

Chapter 6   Derrick Bell, Harvard Law School, and the Emergence of Black Feminist Jurisprudence   123

Chapter 7   Empowerment Within   137

Index   149

About the Author   153

~

Acknowledgments

I would like to thank the following individuals for their help and support with this book. At East Tennessee University I would like to thank Professor Ronnie Day for his contributions to the project, and professors Dorothy Drinkard Hawkshawe, Deborah Harley, Colin Baxter, and Andrew Slap for their support as well. I would also like to thank Professor Robin Means Coleman at the University of Michigan for her kind, strong, and complimentary review of my book. Thanks go out to Daryl Carter, John Kille, and Thomas Young for their support and encouragement of this project as well.

Needless to say a huge thank you goes out to all the law professors—Anita L. Allen, Kimberlé Crenshaw, Lani Guinier, Joyce Hughes, Beverly Moran, Kimberly Jade Norwood, Annette Gordon-Reed, Dorothy Roberts, and Judy Scales Trent. Special thanks goes to Taunya Lovell Banks. Without a doubt you were the inspiration, guidance, and the motivation for me to keep on in my quest to complete this book. May God bless you.

A huge thank you is due to Melissa McNitt at Rowman & Littlefield Publishers for her meticulous attention to detail and her excessive amount of patience as I reworked draft after draft of the manuscript. Thank you to Alan McClare, Douglas Piccinnni, Ruth Gilbert, and Michael McGandy who were also involved with the production and execution of this book.

Finally, I wish to thank my siblings—Bruce, Marsha, Eric, Susan, Steven, and Stephanie—my deceased parents, Elwood and Susan Watson, and my late grandmothers, Mary Beulah and Mazie, who provided me with an unprecedented number of childhood memories.

~

Introduction

On October 11, 1991, University of Oklahoma Law Professor Anita Hill was called before the Senate Judiciary Committee to answer allegations that she had made in a sworn affidavit against Supreme Court nominee Clarence Thomas.[1] For the next few days, the nation was captivated by testimony from numerous individuals in what became known as the Hill-Thomas hearings. Supporters and detractors of Thomas and Hill faced the members of the powerful Judiciary Committee and provided riveting testimony in defense of their party. The hearings left much of the nation spellbound as Hill levied graphic allegations of sexual harassment against Thomas. Doubts about Hill as well as supportive comments were expressed by government officials, media figures, and the general public throughout the hearings. Some detractors accused her of being a race-traitor, a vengeful lesbian, or a feminist pawn used by those who wanted to destroy black men. The level of commentary was intense. On October 15, 1991, the U.S. Senate voted 52–48 in favor of confirming Clarence Thomas to the U.S. Supreme Court. It was the closest margin of victory ever for a Supreme Court nominee.

A year and a half later, on April 29, 1993, when President Bill Clinton nominated University of Pennsylvania Law Professor Lani Guinier for the position of assistant attorney general for civil rights, a political firestorm over her legal writings erupted. In the next several weeks, terms such as "quota queen," "extremely controversial," "tart-tongued black law professor," "black separatist," "fascistic ideology," and "guerrilla warrior" were used to describe Guinier and her ideas. Supporters of Guinier rallied to her defense, charging

1

her conservative critics with smear tactics, dishonesty, distorting her writings, and other unprincipled tactics.[2]

The political atmosphere in the nation's capital became so volatile that it led to the withdrawal of Guinier's nomination by President Clinton on June 3, 1993. Immediately afterward, supporters of Guinier made their displeasure known at how President Clinton had handled her nomination process. The president was charged with being unprincipled, having cold feet, failing to capitalize on an important opportunity for civil rights, being a coward, and depriving a talented African American woman the opportunity to serve the nation.[3] The fact that a previously obscure nominee could cause so much controversy was surprising to most political observers. The fact that President Clinton nominated a black woman law professor for such a prestigious position was even more significant. In the Hill-Thomas hearings, the fact that a black woman law professor would be the key witness against a Supreme Court nominee was newsworthy.

The intersection of race- and gender-oriented scholarship within the legal academy, which Hill's and Guinier's experiences symbolize, is an area of the civil rights movement that has been given some degree of attention. Although in the early 1990s when the *Berkeley Women's Law Journal* explored the topic, hardly any academic material had been written on the subject. One explanation could be the small number of black female law professors in the legal academy. According to Association of American Law Schools statistics for 2001–2002, there were only 222 full-time black female law faculty members. This is in stark contrast to the 1,467 white women and 3,521 white men who are full-time law faculty members.[4]

The playing field in the legal academy is often uneven and frequently excludes black women's values, voices, and vision while embracing the Western patriarchal perspective.[5] The legal academy is another medium for this message to black women. Here race and sex are employed as justification for domination, violence, and destruction. The much maligned, mutilated, and misnamed images—mammy, matriarch, Jezebel, and welfare queen[6]—contribute to their marginal status in the academy. The Eurocentric and androcentric way of devaluing, denigrating, and distorting others' reality is also physically, psychologically, and socially costly to oppressors and oppressed.[7]

Black women's long traditional role in education, as agency, administrator, teacher—in empowering themselves and others—offers a liberating compass for navigating through the multiple "isms" (racism, sexism, classism, etc.) in higher education, as law professor Paulette Caldwell refers to the situation.[8] Many black women legal scholars, in addition to other academics of color, argue that by critiquing European patriarchy, its pedagogies, paradigms, methods, and canons, progressive-oriented scholars can balance the conceptual foundations of the Western scientific mind, which postulates that knowledge can be derived through procedures that are free of race, gender, ethnicity, class, age, or other such contexts.[9]

Since this work primarily concentrates on the generation of black women who entered the legal academy from 1971 to 1992, some historical background is necessary. Three notable pioneers will suffice to illustrate the preceding era. In 1948, Sybil Jones Dedmond was the first black woman to teach full time and to attain tenure in an American law school.[10] Patricia Roberts Harris became a law professor at Howard University in the 1960s. In 1972, Jean Camper Cahn became a cofounder of Antioch Law School and was a pioneer in clinical legal education.[11]

In the fall of 1951, Dedmond, a 1944 graduate of Howard and a 1950 graduate of the University of Chicago Law School, became the first black woman to teach full time in a U.S. law school. She taught criminal law, real estate property, conveyances, and future interests at North Carolina Central University (NCCU). Dedmond remembered her law school experience at Chicago as "comfortable . . . [not] segregating students based on race or sex."[12] She further described Chicago at that time as a "pioneering" school, one with an "exceptionally good atmosphere in which to study law."[13] Dedmond recalled that "there was quite a bit of activism" at Chicago and that it "was one of the more liberal schools where students were intensely involved in political activity."[14]

In the months before her graduation, Dedmond did not interview with white law firms.[15] She worked briefly with a black practitioner in Chicago, doing routine beginning associate work.[16] After a year in practice, she was contacted by a black law school acquaintance, Harry Groves, who had graduated from Chicago in 1949. Groves had been a member of the faculty of North Carolina Central University School of Law, and had decided to enter private practice. He recommended Dedmond as his replacement.[17] She was offered and accepted a faculty position there.[18]

During her first year, her students were all male. The resentments that were often present when black and white women entered previously all male classrooms did not manifest itself in the mixed racial setting of North Carolina in 1950.[19] While at NCCU, Dedmond was actively involved among the community of black lawyers. She joined the pre-oral arguments for some landmark civil rights cases of the 1950s, most notably *Brown v. Board of Education.*[20] She described the experience as one where a congenial group of black lawyers worked together to effectively pursue various strategies.[21] Dedmond remained at NCCU until 1964, then returned to her home town, Pensacola, Florida, to join her husband in private practice.[22]

After some years in private practice and service as a country government administrator, Dedmond returned to teaching as a professor at Pensacola Junior College, where until 1994 she taught courses in the business law curriculum.[23] According to Emma Coleman Jordan, "America's first black female tenured law professor exuded an image of steady, quiet competence. She prospered in the supportive, although restricted, atmosphere of the segregated classrooms of a southern law school." Dedmond acknowledged that she did not endure an arduous time in the legal academy based on race alone or even gender.[24]

Like Dedmond, Patricia Roberts Harris began her career as a law teacher at a predominately black law school.[25] Harris was a lecturer at Howard Law School in the fall of 1961 on a part-time basis.[26] One prominent legal scholar described her as a "tough task master, a teacher who petrified seniors hoping to graduate on time, prompting them to steer clear of her. For those who survived her intellectual challenge, she inspired deep respect and affection."[27]

On February 1, 1969, the Howard University Board of Trustees appointed Harris dean of the law school. Her appointment made her the first black woman in the nation to head a law faculty.[28] But her tenure as dean was short lived; within thirty days she had resigned. Harris had barely warmed the dean's chair when law school students started boycotting classes to protest the war in Vietnam, an issue then rocking the nation.[29] The campus was in a state of siege. For over a week, law students occupied the law building and obstructed classes, causing the university to seek judicial intervention to regain control. After a few weeks, the turmoil on the campus reached a fever pitch. University President James M. Nabrit Jr., under extreme pressure from factions of the university community—students, student leaders, and some faculty and administrators—agreed to meet with students and grant some of their demands. Harris felt that Nabrit had undermined her authority, and subsequently she resigned.[30]

A graduate of Yale Law School, Jean Camper Cahn was another black woman who became a law professor when she founded the Urban Law Institute at George Washington University in 1968.[31] She built her career around the effort to ensure that poor people would receive legal services, and she and her husband, Edgar Cahn, engaged in numerous disputes with the university during their tenure as directors of the Urban Law Institute, which was disbanded in 1971.[32]

The closing of the Urban Law Institute inspired the Cahns to establish the Antioch Law School in 1972.[33] Jean Camper Cahn was the first black woman to create a law school. She and her husband became the thirty-three-year-old co-deans of an institution that many have credited as a pioneer of the clinical teaching method. They "believed that a legal education which was morally neutral on social issues was unacceptable." They wanted to train activists.[34] Although the school had its critics, it obtained full approval from the American Bar Association within three years.[35]

Antioch's highly publicized tenure and subsequent downfall highlight Cahn's qualities and confirmed her contribution to the nascent image of black women law professors. Cahn was a confrontational woman who developed protest methods to further her own agenda.[36] Antioch Law School had been created from the ground up. Students were handpicked for the school.[37] They were expected to dedicate their time and efforts to assisting poor clients and to live with them.[38]

Despite the idealism that guided the enterprise, the once solid structure of the law school disintegrated amid charges of poor management, disputes about control of revenue, and the less than stellar record of Antioch graduates in passing the bar exam. In early 1980, the Cahns were fired by the Antioch board of trustees.[39] Limited in her mobility due to the result of a debilitating stroke, Cahn eventually moved to Florida, where she was counsel to a law firm until her death at age fifty-five.[40] Cahn left a powerful legacy that advocated an unyeilding commitment to helping the poor. Although beset by challenges and reversals of fortune, she never lost her passion for justice.[41]

Despite the pioneering work these women performed in the classroom and in the public sector, their legacies were largely obscure. Aside from a few intellectuals, politicians, and journalists, few Americans knew of these women. Still, the contributions that they made to legal education were significant. Working against the odds, they helped make the legal academy more responsive to the needs of minorities and women.

In 1954, the landmark Supreme Court *Brown v. Board of Education* ruling resulted in the removal of legally sanctioned racial barriers to integrated legal education.[42] Speaking in a unanimous voice, the Warren Court stated in 1954 that it was mandatory that any student, regardless of race or ethnicity, be given access to an equal education. This pronouncement gave legal weight and moral force to an era of social reform and unprecedented federal involvement with the principle of equality as its guide.

The court in *Brown* tried to make the ideas of liberalism a reality for all.[43] Educational opportunity meant equal treatment in a nonsegregated setting.[44] *Brown* laid the groundwork for equality to guide numerous public policy decisions in the years to come. The 1954 decision did not end de facto segregation. However, by eradicating the "separate but equal" underpinning of governmentally sanctioned, forced racial segregation, it set the stage for a fundamental revolution in American law and social patterns. In the years following *Brown*, a number of law schools admitted blacks. The overwhelming majority of blacks admitted to law school were men. By the mid-1960s, more legislation had been enacted to enhance the legal rights of blacks and other minorities in legal education.

In 1964, Congress enacted the Civil Rights Act. Title VII of this act prohibited discrimination on the basis of race, color, and national origin. Applied to education, this provision allayed fears in Congress that federal funds might be spent in support of racially segregated educational programs. Title VII also outlawed gender-based discrimination. This combination of legal provisions provided unprecedented opportunities for women of all races which came to fruition as the 1960s ended.[45]

By the 1970s, a number of law schools began to recruit black men, black women, and white women as students. As the numbers of these groups increased in law schools, so did the demand for black and female law teachers. The increase of minority faculty numbers had to do with the affirmative action policies that were implemented during the Nixon administration.[46] During this decade, the first significant wave of black women began teaching at white law schools. The legal academy began to see cultural diversity as a potential asset.

Paradoxically, a number of institutions in higher education were attacked by white males such as Alan Bakke,[47] Marco DeFunis,[48] and others who claimed to be victims of unfair discrimination. Both cases were pivotal for the institutions of higher education. DeFunis had graduated from the University of Washington at Seattle with a 3.62 grade average.[49] He was accepted by several law schools but desired to stay in Seattle. He applied for admission to the University of Washington Law School in Seattle and was rejected.[50] Consequently, DeFunis took his case to court.

DeFunis was successful in the trial court and was admitted to the law school in 1971. However, the decision was overruled in 1973 by the Washington State Supreme Court, which was strongly in favor of the state affirmative action plan.[51] The U.S. Supreme Court then granted certiorari. By the time the case reached the Supreme Court, DeFunis was in his final semester of law school. Because it was conceded that he would graduate regardless of the outcome, a Supreme Court majority declared the question before it moot.[52] *DeFunis* served as a precedent for the landmark 1978 *Bakke* decision.[53] This case involved a white medical school applicant, Alan Bakke, who charged the University of California at Davis with racial and gender discrimination in its admissions policies when his application was rejected.[54]

As the federal government looked to protect the rights of minorities and women as a matter of justice, a growing number of conservative voices began to demand greater deference to the individual rights of the majority in the name of federalism and political tradition.[55] The extremely conservative Reagan administration tried to dismantle laws demanding equality. The most notable attack on civil rights legislation was an attempt by Republican politicians to repeal the 1965 Voting Rights Act.[56] Throughout the 1980s, the Supreme Court continued to hear cases on race and gender. In 1982, the Court decided against the state of Mississippi in *Mississippi University for Women v. Hogan*.[57] In a 5–4 decision, the Court invalidated the university's all-female admissions policy to its nursing school.

Speaking for the majority, Justice Sandra Day O'Connor articulated an affirmative action rationale with limited applicability to other single-sex admissions policies. She argued that the Court would not necessarily strike down a restriction on admissions that was designed to address the effects of past discrimination.[58] This ruling caused alarm for many advocates of women's rights, particularly for professional black women, and provoked a growing literature on race and gender in the legal academy.[59]

By the late 1980s, the diminishing success of traditional civil rights legal theories, coupled with the mass of black women who were familiar with the writings of black legal scholars and white legal feminists, resulted in the publication of articles by and about black women and the legal system.

In March 1988, sixteen black women professors from law schools in the Northeast began meeting as an informal discussion group. Eventually, the group came to be known as the Northeast Corridor Collective. Founded by Georgetown University Law Professor Emma Coleman-Jordan, this group met once every three months.[60] Membership quadrupled. Its mission was to promote the intersection of racial and gender issues that were of importance to women of color. Their main argument was that women of color have broken new ground by addressing topics that largely only black women treated with academic intensity and rigor. Their argument for racial and gender diversity was a call for academic pluralism.[61]

As the 1990s began, a number of black women in the legal academy became increasingly assertive on social issues. In 1990, a controversy erupted at Harvard Law School that culminated in the publication of an anthology on black women in the legal academy. A black law professor, Derrick Bell, then a senior member of the law faculty at Harvard and a civil rights scholar, announced his intention to protest the lack of faculty diversity by taking an indefinite leave of absence without pay until a woman of color was hired with tenure.

Bell's decision stimulated intense newspaper coverage.[62] News reports contained ample commentary and opinions from black and white students at Harvard, from Harvard faculty, and from faculty of other schools. However, the media seemed largely to ignore the opinions of black women law professors on the controversy.[63] At the time, Regina Austin, a prominent black legal scholar, was a visiting professor at the institution. Due to the ultimatum expressed by Bell, Austin found herself in the middle of a hostile debate.[64] The seeming indifference toward the opinions of black female legal scholars prompted many black women in the legal academy to organize through the Northeast Corridor Collective to publish the anthology "Black Women Law Professors: Building a Community at the Intersection of Race and Gender."[65] The anthology ignited debate among many scholars and brought the issue of diversity to many law journals.[66]

Three ideas emerged as a result of the Bell controversy. First, black women and other women of color brought intellectual diversity to the academy. Second, black women served as role models for black female students in a manner that men of color and white faculty could not.[67] Third, inclusion of women of color in positions of academic leadership enhanced democratic representational ideas.[68]

In light of this background, this book will analyze and discuss the scholarship of a number of black women law professors who have written extensively on the intersection of race and gender from multiple perspectives. The majority of the book will focus on the work of Anita L. Allen, Taunya Lovell Banks, Kimberlé Crenshaw, Lani Guinier, Angela Harris, Cheryl Harris, Anita Hill, Joyce Hughes, Beverly Moran, Kimberly Jade Norwood, Annette Gordon-Reed, Dorothy Roberts, Judy Scales-Trent, and Patricia J. Williams. The work of several other black women law professors will be the subject of reference as well. In addition, this book will examine several issues that have been an integral part of life for women of color in the legal academy and the impact such experiences have had on them as legal scholars. Moreover, it will determine whether the subject of their legal scholarship is substantially different from that of white men, black men, and white feminists.

Chapter 1 discusses two black women law professors in the media spotlight—Anita Hill and Lani Guinier—and the reaction they received from the media, their colleagues, and the public at large.

Chapter 2 focuses on the often hostile and unsupportive work environment and other obstacles that black women law professors in the legal academy have historically faced from others who have been uncomfortable with their presence.

Chapter 3 looks at the multiple isms—racism, sexism, elitism, and other isms—that many black women law professors in the legal academy routinely endure and the mechanisms they employ for coping with them.

Chapter 4 explores the impact that the issue of affirmative action has had on a number of these women and the stereotypes and assumptions that many of their white colleagues harbor about them as beneficiaries of the policy.

Chapter 5 examines the often complex relationships that several law professors have discussed in dealing with their students, and it looks at the environment of the legal academy that many professors believe has contributed to such an ambiguous relationship.

Chapter 6 discusses the formation of the Northeast Corridor Collective by a group of black women law professors from northeastern law schools in 1988 and how the scholarship better known as black feminist jurisprudence emerged from this meeting.

Chapter 7 looks at the current state of affairs as well as the future outlook for black women in the legal academy.

Black women law professors have endured numerous obstacles, internal as well as external, in an environment that frequently has been less than cordial. Their story is a complex one.

Notes

1. Edwin Chen and Paul Houston, "Senate Delays Vote on Thomas to Probe Harassment Charges," *L.A. Times*, October 9, 1991, A1.

2. Bob Cohn, "Crowning a Quota Queen?" *Newsweek*, May 24, 1993, 67.

3. Linda Wright Moore, "The Chance She Never Got," *Philadelphia Daily News*, June 10, 1993.

4. Richard White, AALS Law School Statistics, 2001–2002.

5. Patricia J. Williams, *The Alchemy of Race and Rights: The Diary of a Law Professor* (Cambridge, MA: Harvard University Press, 1991).

6. K. Sue Jewell, *From Mammy to Miss America and Beyond: Cultural Images and the Shaping of U.S. Social Policy* (New York: Routledge, 1993).

7. Lois Benjamin, *Black Women in the Academy: Promises and Perils* (Gainesville: University of Florida Press, 1997).

8. Interview with Paulette Caldwell, March 26, 1997.

9. Benjamin, *Black Women in the Academy*, 6.

10. Emma Coleman-Jordan, "Images of Black Women in the Legal Academy: An Introduction," *Berkeley Women's Law Journal* 6 (Winter–Spring 1990–1991): 11–13.

11. J. Clay Smith, *Rebels in Law: Voices in History of Black Women Lawyers* (Ann Arbor: University of Michigan Press, 1998), 279–80.

12. Coleman-Jordan, "Images of Black Women," 13.

13. Coleman-Jordan, "Images of Black Women," 13.

14. Coleman-Jordan, "Images of Black Women," 13.

15. Coleman-Jordan, "Images of Black Women," 13.

16. Coleman-Jordan, "Images of Black Women," 13.

17. Coleman-Jordan, "Images of Black Women," 13.

18. Coleman-Jordan, "Images of Black Women," 13.

19. Coleman-Jordan, "Images of Black Women," 13.

20. 377 US (1954).

21. Richard Kluger, *Simple Justice: The History of Brown v. Board of Education and Black America's Struggle for Equality* (New York: Knopf, 1975).

22. Coleman-Jordan, "Images of Black Women," 14.

23. Coleman-Jordan, "Images of Black Women," 14.

24. Coleman-Jordan, "Images of Black Women," 14.

25. J. Clary Smith Jr., "Patricia Roberts Harris: A Champion in Pursuit of Excellence," *Howard Law Journal* 29 (1986): 437, 447.

26. "New Officials Named," *Howard University Magazine*, November 5, 1961.

27. Coleman-Jordan, "Images of Black Women," 15–17.

28. "Patricia Harris Is New Law School Dean," *Howard University Newsletter*, February 24, 1969.

29. Elizabeth Shelton, "Top Lady Lonely at Howard," *Washington Post*, February 20, 1969.

30. Smith, "Patricia Harris Roberts," 449, 450.

31. Alice Bonner, "The Controversial Cahns," *Washington Post*, May 26, 1982.

32. Coleman-Jordan, "Images of Black Women," 19.

33. Courtland Milloy, "A Passion for Justice That Never Waned," *Washington Post*, February 17, 1991.

34. Milloy, "A Passion for Justice."

35. Jean Camper Cahn, "Tribute to George Strait," *Iowa Law Review* 70 (1985): 754, 758.

36. Jacqueline Trescott, "Pros and Cahns: Controversy's Old Pros: The Cahns; Triumph and Turmoil, the Constant Companion of Antioch's Rebels," *Washington Post*, January 19, 1980.

37. Coleman-Jordan, "Images of Black Women," 18–19.

38. Coleman-Jordan, "Images of Black Women," 18–19.

39. Trescott, "Pros and Cahns."

40. Milloy, "A Passion for Justice."

41. Coleman-Jordan, "Images of Black Women," 20.

42. *Brown v. Board of Education of Topeka, Kansas,* 347 U.S. (1954).

43. Kluger, *Simple Justice,* 748–53.

44. Rosemary C. Salomone, *Equal Education under Law: Legal Rights and Federal Policy in the Post-Brown Era* (New York: St. Martin's, 1986), 3–8.

45. Salomone, *Equal Education,* 3–8.

46. Dean J. Kotlowski, "Richard Nixon and the Origins of Affirmative Action," *Historian* 60 (Spring 1998): 523–41.

47. *Regents of the University of California v. Bakke*, 438 U.S. 265 (1978).

48. *DeFunis v. Odegaard*, 416 U.S. 312 (1974).

49. *DeFunis v. Odegaard*, 507 P.2d 1194, 82 Wash. 2d 11 (1973).

50. *DeFunis v. Odegaard*, 1181 (1973).

51. *DeFunis v. Odegaard*, 1169 (1973).

52. *DeFunis v. Odegaard*, 312, 317, 348, 350 (1974).

53. J. Harvie Wilkinson, *From Brown to Bakke: The Supreme Court and School Integration, 1954–1978* (New York: Oxford University Press, 1979), 245–61.

54. *Regents of the University of California v. Bakke*, 438 U.S. 265 (1978).

55. Salomone, *Equal Education under Law*, 10.

56. 457 U.S. (1965).

57. 458 U.S. 718 (1982).

58. 458 U.S. 728.

59. Paula Giddings, *When and Where I Enter: The Impact of Black Women on Race and Sex in America* (New York: Bantam, 1984).

60. Interview with Emma Coleman-Jordan, February 24, 1997.

61. Interview with Emma Coleman-Jordan, February 24, 1997.

62. Fox Butterfield, "Old Rights Campaigner Leads a Harvard Battle," *New York Times*, May 21, 1990.

63. Coleman-Jordan, "Images of Black Women," 4.

64. Fox Butterfield, "Harvard Law School Torn by Race Issue," *New York Times*, April 25, 1990.

65. "Black Women Law Professors: Building a Community at the Intersection of Race and Gender, A Symposium," *Berkeley Women's Law Journal* 6 (Winter–Spring 1990–1991).

66. Richard H. Chused, "The Hiring and Retention of Minorities and Women on American Law School Faculties," University of Pennsylvania Law Review 137:2 (1988): 537, 539.

67. Anita Allen, "On Being a Role Model," *Berkeley Women's Law Journal* 6 (Winter–Spring 1990–1991): 30–36.

68. Allen "On Being a Role Model," 30–36.

CHAPTER ONE

~

In the Media Spotlight:
Anita Hill and Lani Guinier

In the early 1990s, two black women law professors became prominent in the public eye—Anita Hill and Lani Guinier. Both women received nationwide attention during this time period. Both managed to see their pasts confront them in a brutal manner. One became a plaintiff of sorts, and the other became a defendant.

On October 18, 1991, Clarence Thomas was appointed as the 106th justice of the U.S. Supreme Court. He would become the Court's second African American justice, replacing the legendary Thurgood Marshall. The nomination process involved weeks of televised confirmation hearings, riveting debate among the public and media pundits, and the final Senate vote. More than fifteen years later, the hearings are still the subject of heated debate, particularly in a number of liberal and conservative political circles. In the initial months after Thomas's confirmation, syndicated columnists, television and magazine journalists, academics, and others provided considerable material about the hearings. In many ways, the hearings set the agenda for the 1990s. Lack of diversity, white male domination, sexism, sexual harassment, and other issues that had been previously marginalized now were debated on center stage for the first time. Even more interesting was the fact that these issues were brought to the forefront by two black women.

Before the hearings began, Thomas was set to be easily confirmed by the Senate Judiciary Committee to take a seat on the Supreme Court. Then an allegation hit the mainstream media like a napalm bomb. Leaked to National Public Radio and *Newsday* was the information that Anita Hill, a black law professor at the University of Oklahoma, had given a confidential affidavit to the Senate Judiciary Committee and a report to the FBI that Thomas had sexually harassed her some ten years earlier when she worked with him at the Department of Education and later at the Equal Employment Opportunity Commission (EEOC). Anita Hill's dramatic testimony brought a thundering halt to a confirmation that had seemed all but assured.[1]

Millions of Americans now heard details of a sordid kind in a drama featuring two ivy-league-educated black Americans (they both had Yale degrees) and a cast of impressive supporting actors representing the political left and right. Not about to be left out of this dramatic potpourri was a significant number of people who belonged to the national press corps.[2] Soon lobbyists, attorneys, professors, and some corporate heads became involved with the hearings. Demonstrators from all walks of life, former classmates and colleagues of Hill and Thomas, their family members and neighbors became involved. From the start, those who were most involved or touched by the case groped for words to characterize the hearings—"a circus" was one of Thomas's milder appellations. A number of congressmen referred to the hearings as "painful" and "horrendous."[3]

Anita Hill was accompanied into the Senate chambers by prominent African American female legal scholars Taunya Lovell Banks, Kimberlé Crenshaw, and Emma Coleman-Jordan.[4] Hill's charges threatened Thomas's confirmation in a manner that his EEOC record on the aged, his silence on *Roe v. Wade*[5] (which Senator Joseph Biden of Delaware called "the most artful dodge I have ever seen"), and considerable apprehension in regard to his suitability to become a member of the nation's highest court failed to do.[6] Once the charges were made public and Senate hearings were called, dramatic debate began across the country in bars, college campuses, law firms, private homes, houses of worship, parties, weekend retreats, upscale suburbs, downtown districts, small-town America, and virtually all avenues of American society about what really happened between these two high-achieving African Americans, and most importantly, which one of them had the truth on their side.[7] Even now, more than fifteen years later, the hearings still touch a raw nerve with a number of Americans.

From the outset of the bombshell revelations until well after the hearings concluded on October 15, 1991, it was the main topic wherever people gathered. Several years later, in her book *Speaking Truth to Power*, Hill described her life-changing experience: "People of all ages, races, and backgrounds wrote. Just about every category of person imaginable who had seen, heard, or read about the hearing took time to put their reactions into words. Some letters were from old friends who wanted to reconnect after years of no communication, but most were from strangers expressing their concern about what they had witnessed." Hill further stated:

> In the quiet of my office, after classes were over and most of the staff had left, I tried to read at least forty letters a day. Many, especially those from harassment victims, were heart-wrenching. Because of their intensity and my fatigue, reading my assigned number of letters at the end of a workday often proved impossible. I would become despondent and unable to continue, or angered by my own helplessness to change things. I changed my routine, setting aside time to read mail the first thing in the morning. But this was a mistake because after reading of all the embarrassment, anger and grief, I could not focus on my work. This letter speaking of abuse or that letter describing disillusionment stayed with me all the day.[8]

She was also quick to acknowledge that among the letter writers were detractors who did not hesitate to express their hostility: "Though there were the threatening, vulgar, and just plain cruel messages, they were few and I thank God for that. So as not to delude myself into believing that everyone saw my testimony in a positive light, I read them as well. The outrage I felt over the abusive experiences described in some of the letters numbed me to any cruelty my detractors could dish out. In the face of so much pain, their hostility seemed trivial."[9]

While there was certainly hostility, resentment, paranoia, and suspicion from all quarters of American society—conservatives, liberals, men, women—nowhere were emotions of horror, disbelief, disillusionment, and hostility more riled than in the African American community.[10] It is safe to say that virtually the entire African American community was blindsided by what was taking place. The hearings became a tawdry, perverted, ugly media spectacle for the entire world to see. Moreover, the two objects of attention were black.[11] Rather than being able to take immense pride in witnessing two African Americans who should have been seen as individuals who had achieved considerable success in their respective fields, what was playing out (at least in the minds of a large number of African Americans) was the "airing of dirty laundry" that should have been kept behind closed doors, safely out of the reach of a white public that was often too eager to perceive pathologies in the African American community.[12]

A sense of profound embarrassment engulfed much of the community.[13] Others felt disgusted, ashamed, and degraded at hearing overt, frank, graphic references to sex and pornography.[14] Many African Americans believed that such graphic, lurid talk about the alleged sexual harassment provided perverse ammunition for the long-held, misleading stereotypes of black people as sexually immature, perverted, and unhinged. However, in reality, there has always been a strong streak of conservatism among many black people in regard to sexual politics.[15] Historically speaking, in much of the black community, it was taboo to discuss sexual behavior in public.[16] Needless to say, it was much more unacceptable to do so in front of an audience of millions of white Americans.[17] At a time when so many African Americans were facing a plethora of critical social and political issues, that a case of rabid sexual allegations between two African Americans was the focus of intense debate made many in the community disgusted.[18] Legal scholar Kimberlé Crenshaw argues that the embracing of Thomas and the demonizing of Hill was due to historical practices within the black community that have long marginalized gender domination to struggle against racial oppression. Crenshaw further argued that because of this, the particular experiences of black men have often been seen as "the black experience" as was demonstrated by the ammunition and perverse security that Thomas gained by employing the lynching metaphor and the marginalization of representations of black female domination.[19]

As more details of the charges and the history of Thomas's and Hill's relationship became public, it was almost impossible for a black adult male or female to not have an opinion on the issue. I saw such a drama play out in my own family. And there was no consensus among blacks. The differences sometimes fell along gender lines. Within the black community, both Thomas and Hill had men and women who were adamant supporters and ardent detractors. The positions taken by African Americans demonstrated the powerful intersection of race and gender and the impact it had on the black community.[20] As one law professor stated: "The characters' debate over the credibility of Thomas and Hill strikingly echoed the actual discussions that had occurred in the media. Race and gender each were powerful symbols, present on the show as they had been in the media during the hearings. Yet the intersection of the two, made relevant by the very existence of Hill—an African American woman—was rendered invisible both in the hearings and by the media coverage."[21]

Almost all issues and depictions that have been paramount to black male–female relationships emerged to the forefront: the image of the black male sexual predator, the gratuitous meddling of white feminists, marriage across the color line, and the ardent belief that black women should demonstrate their unwavering support for black men especially in the face of white opposition.[22] When the final Senate roll call was taken at the end of the hearings, Clarence Thomas was confirmed by 52 to 48 votes. It was the closest margin of victory ever for a Supreme Court justice. As the decade progressed, public sentiment on the hearings shifted considerably, with Anita Hill gaining more supporters.[23]

One question for debate is why were so many in the African American community increasingly hostile to Anita Hill from the moment her charges were aired until the final Senate count? The primary reason is that Hill was seen as doing the "dirty work" of the white power structure.[24] In many quarters of the African American community, white conservatives, white feminists, and other white "special interest" groups are seen as the "enemy," particularly among black men.[25] Such a mindset has deep historical roots. From various attempts at social emasculation, to lynchings, to the current high levels of incarceration, African American males have been the primary victims of white racism.[26] Black women have been expected to stand alongside and support black men. For a long time this has been an unwritten rule of the black community. Moreover, it has been a role that black women had accepted without question until the late 1960s.[27] One of the main reasons black women accepted the role of comforter so readily was an acknowledgement that white men perceived black men as a major physical threat.[28] Black women have generally had an easier time navigating through the white power structure than their male cohorts.[29] Even after the challenges and ideas that the modern women's movement promoted regarding sexual equality, the pattern of black women adhering to the wishes of black men was considered the appropriate thing to do. Black women who resisted this traditional power structure were often branded as traitors, man-haters, Jezebels, Sapphires, or abnormal.[30] Truth be told, such labels have been commonplace in the white community as well. Legendary historian Nell Irvin Painter argued that Clarence Thomas did not hesitate to manipulate this historical fact to his advantage.[31]

There has been a long, historical belief among many black Americans that there is a conspiracy by the dominant white society to denigrate and marginalize black men.[32] This belief is supported by the sobering statistics on the economic, educational, and health status of blacks in the United States. In the early and mid 1990s, the number of prominent African American men who were under public scrutiny further confirmed suspicions among many black Americans.[33] In her 1993 article "The Witch Hunt," Mary A. Fischer reports, "of the 465 political-corruption probes initiated between 1983 and 1988, 14 percent targeted black officials, though they made up only 3 percent of all U.S. officeholders. . . . In the [U.S.] House of Representatives, . . . roughly half of the then twenty-six members of the Congressional Black Caucus were the target of federal investigations and/or indictments between 1981 and 1993. For the number to be equal for white representatives, 204 of the 409 white House members would have been subjected to the same scrutiny during that time, yet according to Justice Department figures, only 15 actually were."[34]

In his 1992 article "Sex, Lies, and Stereotypes," Sylvester Monroe notes that Clarence Thomas, Marion Barry, Mike Tyson, Rick James, pop superstar Michael Jackson, football hall of fame player O. J. Simpson, actors Jim Brown and Eddie Murphy, former Illinois Congressman Gus Savage, *Washington Post* journalist Juan Williams, conservative commentator Armstrong Williams, NBA superstar Alan Iverson, Jesse Jackson, and baseball powerhouse Barry Bonds had all been accused of either sexual abuse, infidelity, or sexual misconduct.[35] Sadly, in the case of some of these men, the allegations turned out to be true. Taken together, these journalistic accounts lend credence to the African American community's conspiracy theory. It is the belief among a large segment of the African American community that negative news, and particularly negative news about African American men, sells. Anyone—especially a black woman—who is perceived as "targeting a black man" is thought to be working on the side of the conspirators.[36]

Journalist Elsie Washington argued that in the Hill-Thomas case, Hill was considered by many to be either a (witting or unwitting) tool of the senators, white feminists, and other whites who opposed Thomas's (or any other black man's) ascension to the vacant Supreme Court seat. Some blacks drew comparisons to Hazel "Rasheeda" Moore, in the Marion Barry drug case; Desiree Washington, in the charge against Tyson; and Mary Stansel, whose lawsuit resulted in the NAACP's ouster of Benjamin Chavis in 1994.[37] Anita Hill described her own experiences:

> Yet in 1991 that community, the source of my social and psychological identity from childhood became the source of my greatest discomfort. Voices in the community rose to condemn me for committing a community sin—bearing witness against a Black man made all the worse because my protest involved matters of sexuality. For the first time in my life, I began to question my place in the Black community and its place in my life. Nevertheless, in this letter, I saw not simply the community's condemnation but an affirmation of my continued membership in it.[38]

Hill, who went to great lengths to find exactly the right words to express her allegation, faced a deep dilemma. Despite the fact that she was apprehensive about how much detail she wanted to go into, once she decided to go forth with her testimony she expected that the members of the senate judiciary committee would grant her the courtesy of a public hearing.[39] A number of white conservative senators, Democrats as well as Republicans, were vicious in their attacks on Hill. Alabama Senator Howell Heflin asked Hill if she was "interested in writing a book," was "delusional," or suffered from a "martyr complex."[40] Pennsylvania Senator Arlen Specter argued that Anita Hill's testimony amounted to "flat out perjury."[41] Such an assumption of opportunism was quickly discredited by others who were intimate with Hill. Her colleague at the University of Oklahoma School of Law, Shirley Wiegand, argued: "Anita Hill was not taken with the advice of any interest groups . . . we felt it was very dangerous to accept help from them. That was not what she had in mind. Later, when the folks [from interest groups] started trying to get involved, she made it clear that she didn't want them involved. She knew that would be misinterpreted. She doesn't align herself with political factions. She still doesn't call herself a feminist."[42]

Hill was also denounced for the timing of her revelations: opponents argued that she had not taken her complaints to the appropriate parties or confronted Thomas himself about his behavior in 1981 or 1982. In "Public Hearing, Private Pain," a documentary about the case shown on television's *Frontline*, a considerable number of black women who were interviewed believed that Hill should have kept silent and let bygones be bygones. The fact that her allegations may have been credible made no difference in their opinion that she should not have brought the matter up if she had let so many years pass without discussing the incident with anyone else.[43]

The fact that Anita Hill was a well-educated, well-heeled black woman, and not like the images that society has attributed to black women, made it difficult for many white men, particularly the white male Senate Judiciary Committee, to embrace her. As the distinguished scholar of the black woman's experience Nellie McKay noted:

> Because Anita Hill is Black and a Woman, but fits none of the stereotypes of Black women to which Black women are accustomed (the mammy, the slut, the virago, etc.), these men could find no reference point for her, and therefore she had no believability for them. That is why some had to make her over themselves, imposing on her other images more comfortable for them.[44]

Hill recited harrowing accounts of the tension that existed between her and many senators on the committee. She recounted how several of them, in particular Arlen Specter of Pennsylvania, would repeat the same question over and over again until he received the response he wanted. Outraged by his lack of respect, she decided that she would not relent to his agenda and allow him to put words into her mouth. She was determined to take a combative stance at all costs. In *Speaking Truth to Power*, Hill admitted that some of the bantering that took place between her and Specter may have looked foolish to the press, but in some ways, it garnered her a certain degree of satisfaction.[45] According to Hill,

> The ease with which I was transformed from respected academician to malicious psychotic in the eyes of the public illustrates the tenuousness of my association with power. In sum, my license to speak before the committee as a credible witness was revoked by the tribunal and the process. I was cast aside as just another African American woman who was not to be trusted to describe her own experiences truthfully and who had no place in the decidedly political arena of the moment.[46]

She further argued:

> It was this reconstruction of me—a portrait of a dangerous, unbelievable, ambitious, disappointed woman—that the senators used to justify the warning to "watch out for Anita Hill." The portrait was further reinforced by the retelling of the stories of Janet Cooke and Tawana Brawley by some commentators and editorial writers.[47] Various senators and their collaborators struggled to place me as far outside the norms of proper behavior as they could, painting me as simultaneously prudish yet lewd, easily duped yet shrewd and ambitious, fantasizing yet calculating, pathetic yet evil.[48]

Hill recounted at length how Clarence Thomas's supporters enlisted many factions, including some of her former students, in an effort to discredit her.

> Thomas supporters sought out students who would provide statements asserting that I was a radical feminist, a lesbian, a sexual aggressor, or an incompetent teacher. Senator Danforth's campaign included calling several of my former students ten to twelve times over the course of two days. Yet even with the breadth of his inquiry and the persistence of his search, Senator Danforth was able to obtain only one affidavit, the contents of which were denied by the "witnesses" listed in the document. This affidavit was dubbed the "pube affidavit" because it contained descriptions of alleged sexual remarks, advances, and bizarre activity including putting pubic hair in student papers I returned—that the former student attributed to me. The alleged remarks, according to the document, were made in the presence of the students named in the affidavit. But when the Senate contacted those named students, they denied witnessing any such activity.[49]

In the initial months following the hearings, Anita Hill received little sympathy from the American public. Sexual harassment, while acknowledged, had not been an issue much discussed in the larger American community, especially, the African American community.[50] Several callers left obscene messages on Hill's answering machine.[51] A male civil rights leader called her to argue that Thomas's behavior was normal for a black man.[52] Sisters should stand by their brothers, many said. As one writer explained it later,

> Hill confronted and ultimately breached a series of taboos in the Black community that have survived both slavery and the post-segregation life she and Clarence Thomas share. Anita Hill put her private business in the street, and she downgraded a Black man to a room filled with White men who might alter his fate—surely a large enough betrayal for her to be read out of the race.[53]

Sexual harassment was an issue that was discussed behind closed doors, and the perception was that only "really dirty old men," not "respectable men," engaged in this sort of behavior. Legal scholars Adrienne Davis and Stephanie Wildman argued:

> After the allegations brought by Anita Hill became public, many watched in disbelief, realizing that our representative institution was in fact filled with people who did not or would not comprehend the substance and standards of sex discrimination law. As they proved in their comments to the press and in their questioning of Hill, few, if any, members of the Senate Judiciary Committee know what constitutes sexual harassment. Senator Alan Simpson distinguished sexual harassment from "real harassment." Senator Arlen Specter was unsure whether speech without physical contact was included in its ambit. The most elite electoral institution found itself floundering hopelessly when attempting to face the issue of sexism, a problem that plagues more than half of the country's citizens. Consequently, because the senators could not fathom the issue of sexism from their ocean of privilege, they certainly could not understand the intersection of sexism with racism.[54]

Indeed, as Elsie Washington and others note, some black men argue that sexual banter between African American men and women has been a fact of life (as it has been between whites and interracially).[55] Harvard University sociology professor Orlando Patterson went so far as to argue that Clarence Thomas's behavior toward Anita Hill was nothing more than a style of "down home courting."[56] Not only does Patterson's "analysis" place the fault of sexual harassment with the victim, but such a nonchalant response is dangerous on several levels. His naïve commentary demonstrates his misunderstanding of black American cultural mores (this could be due to his Caribbean upbringing). Even worse, his misguided, retrograde belief that it was acceptable to engage in crude, obscene, sexual innuendo toward black women is the sort of mentality that often enables sexual misconduct and violence against women. Such a view has also helped perpetuate a gender hierarchy. More than a few black women have acknowledged that receiving this kind of crude sexual banter from men on the street and at work has been such a common occurrence that they by default accepted it as the norm.[57] In fact, several of the law professors interviewed for this book recited experiences where they had been the victims of sexual harassment or unwanted propositions by both black and white men at some point in their careers. Personal experiences aside, the fact is that most black women consider raw, bawdy, sexually trumped up comments by men on the street to be an insulting act of sexual violation they would rather not have to endure.[58]

Until the Hill-Thomas hearings heightened the country's awareness of how women might feel about lewd remarks from men who were total strangers, black women in general had not publicly discussed the way they were treated and viewed by black males.[59] Outside of occasional books and newspaper articles, there were few public arenas for black women to voice their concerns on the issues about black men that they viewed as problematic.[60] In 1991, the CBS television program *Designing Women* dedicated an episode to "The Strange Case of Clarence and Anita." This particular episode addressed the intersection of politics, pop culture, and contemporary cultural mores. The issues that were discussed in the show revolved around the intersection of race and gender that were paramount during the hearings.[61]

Throughout the years, a number of academics have discussed the episode at length. A number of them, such as Stephanie Wildman and Adrienne Davis, argue that while the producers should be commended for producing such an episode, there are several problematic factors with the episode, which in all probability was unconsciously racist. One problem was that there were five white women and one black man discussing the Hill-Thomas case. Thus, there was a complete absence of the perspective of a black woman. Throughout the episode, Anita Hill's face is shown, but the audience does not hear her voice. Rather, we hear the opinions of five white women and a black man. Ironically, much like the Senate hearings, Hill's voice was minimized in that her views were represented by white women and a black man, who was also marginalized, as opposed to Hill herself. Moreover, this particular episode unwittingly promoted long-held stereotypes about black men when the black male character responded to a question about the supposedly well-endowed black male and other historically racially charged themes in the episode.[62]

Anita Hill has said it was not her intention to become a poster child for the issue of sexual harassment, but circumstances resulted in that being the case. Her disappointment on how events culminated is evident in her remarks about meeting with members of the press:

In the statement, as in responding to questions, I tried to urge upon the press that in sending my statement to the U.S. Senate I had responded to the inquiry of a senate staffer, that I was not acting to raise a sexual harassment claim but out of my sense of responsibility to the nomination process, and that I felt the senate had an obligation to resolve the matter, since some of its members had already responded to the reports of my charges by impugning my integrity. This was the first time I asked for a public resolution, but at that moment I knew if there was none, I would certainly live under the shadow of the accusations of fabrications forever. Even with a public resolution, the shadow might well continue for years. Without a chance to address publicly the allegations of those who called me liar, I would spend my entire life addressing them privately. I wanted the matter resolved "so much that all of you nice people can just go home," I concluded. We all laughed nervously.[63]

Hill did not hesitate to attack the press for what she saw as their less than professional approach in reporting the story and what she perceived to be a bias in favor of Clarence Thomas by segments of the mainstream media.

A 1992 *Columbia Journalism Review* study showed that the press coverage was biased in favor of Thomas, with his proponents quoted three times more often than those who favored a hearing on my claim. Thomas' family life and personal background were explored quite positively by the press for weeks prior to the leak. Before the hearings, the press gave little attention to my background. The *New York Times* carried a major story about me featuring a photograph of my parents, but it was the only paper to do so. Only after the hearings did the press explore my background, and then only to prove or disprove this or that theory about my charges. With nothing to contradict them, hostile senators could portray me in any manner they chose. Once the hearings started, those same senators could paint my claim as bizarre or aberrant and therefore incredible, since credible information about sexual harassment was also absent from the press coverage.[64]

In an interview that was conducted a few months after the hearings, Anita Hill stated, "As African-American women, we are always trained to value our community even at the expense of ourselves. . . . We are constrained from expressing our negative experiences because they are perceived in the larger community as a bad reflection on African Americans. . . . It's an unfortunate and awful position for Black women to be in. It's interesting that people haven't seen the harassment of Black women as a betrayal."[65]

In her book *Speaking Truth to Power*, Hill described a public scene that she was involved in:

But accepting the hard fact that I became a symbol of an issue and had thus lost something of my right to privacy was not enough. I had to accept being treated by people as less than human. I had become the female counterpart of Ralph Ellison's "*Invisible Man*." I was obvious, but my humanity was not—like a figure it was not—like a figure in a wax museum to be admired, poked, gazed at, and photographed. Or insulted. Once a young couple in front of me at a counter began to speak about me in intentionally audible whispered tones. "Yes, that is her," he said. "Well, I just know she lied," she responded. "Look at her. I can't believe she has the nerve to be seen in public," she said. Finally, exasperated, I remarked that it was rude of them to "whisper" right in front of me. In a bizarre response, he referred to his friend: "We were just talking about the time she was raped." I retreated, realizing that anyone with so little sensitivity as to personalize rape and speak of it so glibly would have no qualms about offending me or anyone else.[66]

Anita Hill was an easy target for some of the more vicious detractors. She was a single woman in a major metropolitan area, Washington, D.C., a city where single professional women outnumber single professional men by a large margin. This is a fact that is duplicated in most large metropolitan areas where large numbers of black Americans reside.[67] That Clarence Thomas had been married to an African American woman, divorced her, and then dated and wed a white woman further stoked the opinions of the conspiracy chattering class. One of the hallmark beliefs in American society is that African American women hold nothing but contempt for African American men who date or marry outside their race. Rumor had it that Anita Hill was resentful at having to endure dismissive attitudes that African American women have often faced from black men who choose white women to mate with.[68] Virginia Thomas, wife of Clarence Thomas, told *People* magazine that "Anita Hill was probably in love with my husband."[69] In *Speaking Truth to Power*, Hill explained the psychological and emotional toll such an experience had on her:

> What happened in October 1991 should not have happened to me or anyone else. Nevertheless, it did, and is now such an integral part of who I am that I cannot imagine how my life would be today if it hadn't. My life has been forever changed. I will never again feel as safe and secure as I did before I received the first threats on my life. One day recently in a supermarket in Norman, a friend came up behind me, without identifying himself, and put his hands over my eyes. I panicked and for hours afterward was shaken at the act and the fear it brought to the surface. I reacted in the same way when, two years after the hearing, an NBC news crew rushed toward me in my driveway seeking a comment on the endowed professorship.[70]

A few months following the hearings, journalist David Brock wrote a blistering attack on Hill in an article entitled "The Real Anita Hill," published in the conservative *American Spectator*, a magazine known in some political cir-cles as the most "anti-Clinton magazine in America." Anyone who was close to or associated with President Bill Clinton was a target for the magazine. The article was mostly a psychoanalysis of the supposed dysfunctional behavior of Anita Hill by a number of her associates. The article showed an extremely racist depiction of Hill with large protruding lips extending considerable length. One of the most memorable quotes of the article that became common gossip in all political circles was that Hill was "a bit nutty and a bit slutty."[71] The line was employed by conservative commentators such as Rush Limbaugh, Don Imus, and Neal Boortz, to name a few. Indeed, it seemed that many white male conservative commentators had no problem engaging in vicious assaults on an African American woman. In response to Brock, Hill argued:

> David Brock is a product of the times in which we live now. As a White male he is given permission to define me, a Black woman, on whatever terms he chooses, without establishing any credentials to do so. He is presumed to be free of bias, no matter how obviously biased his work may be. Many accept his claim to sources without reference to who they are or what their bias may be. . . . None of the critics questioned why a woman, as ambitious and politically and sexually aggressive as the woman portrayed by Brock, would ever go to Ok-lahoma to teach at an unaccredited, conservative, Christian law school. No one ever asked why that same aggressive, ambitious character would wait ten years to "get Clarence Thomas."[72]

Several years later, in his book *Blinded by the Right: The Conscience of an Ex-Conservative*, which was a scathing attack on many of his former friends on the political right, Brock admitted that he "lied about Anita Hill" and sev-eral other people who were targets of the conservative right, and he publicly apologized to her.[73]

When I interviewed legal scholar Kimberlé Crenshaw in 1999, she dis-cussed the Hill-Thomas controversy at length. According to Crenshaw, the Hill-Thomas hearings demonstrate how devastating gender divisions can be to the interests of the black community. Initially, before the hearings, African Americans were ambivalent about Clarence Thomas. However, when the hearings were televised and the allegations about his behavior be-came public, many African Americans saw him as a victim of racism. Be-cause of this, Thomas was able to easily manipulate black public opinion by wrapping himself into a history of lynching, which is a clearly racially in-flected history.[74]

In Crenshaw's view, when black people heard Thomas's message about a "high-tech lynching" and then gathered around him, what they were doing was acting on a gendered experience of racial oppression, without even being aware that they were rejecting another gendered experience of racial oppression, namely the long history of black women being vulnerable to a certain kind of sexual assault and harassment and their experiences being completely and utterly marginalized and dismissed. For the most part, there is no outlet for a black woman to make such a charge and be identified as a victim worthy of the community's support. Yet Clarence Thomas was allowed a platform to make this exact argument. Because of this situation, many in the black community came to the conclusion that he deserved our support, and Anita Hill did not. Thomas, in essence, was a racial victim who was cast into a hero by the black community. The community then supported his quest to earn a seat on the Supreme Court. Unlike Thomas, Anita Hill was cast as a she-devil, a female Judas of sorts, who deserved to be isolated from the community.

Ironically, since taking his seat on the Supreme Court, Thomas has voted in a manner that has been vehemently detrimental to the interests of African Americans. On more than one case, Thomas's vote has made the difference on whether African Americans received educational resources or not, and whether black Americans will have a voting rights act that keeps up with the strategies white conservatives use to weaken black voting power. Thomas has voted against the argument that innocence is a justifiable defense against the application of the death penalty. One vote after another, he has done everything he can to weaken black political interests in this country, Crenshaw finds.

Just knowing they had the ability to support or even strengthen their demands through the courts was a huge factor, both legally and psychologically, for black Americans, Crenshaw noted. They knew there was a significant chance to negotiate and win. During Thomas's tenure on the Court, however, many of the demands that African Americans saw as crucial were instead viewed as trivial and not worthy of support. "To be frank," Crenshaw argued, "one really has to ask what was it about the black community's reaction that made that happen, because I am totally clear that if it were not for broad support of the African American community, Clarence would not have gotten all the votes that he needed."[75]

Many senators have been loyal to African American voters due to Jesse Jackson's voting registration in the 1988 presidential election, which brought significant numbers of black voters to the polls and got Democrats elected in the white South when Republicans were gaining considerable inroads in the region. Black people voted those politicians into office. These were the same politicians saying that they would like to vote against this guy, but that the faxes they were receiving, the newspaper stories they were reading, and the opinion polls they were watching demonstrated to them that the African American community was solidly in support of Thomas, Crenshaw noted. What you had, Crenshaw says, was a situation where black people were supporting someone not because of what he had actually done, and without looking at who supported him. That senators such as Strom Thurmond, an arch segregationist, supported Clarence Thomas should have given the black community pause. Crenshaw believed that if the black community had looked at some of the groups and individuals who were supporting Clarence Thomas, they would not have been so adamant in their support of him. Instead, what they saw was a black woman trying to bring down a black man.

The mentality in much of the community was that of course we must stand up for him, Crenshaw noted. As she explained, many African Americans did not realize that by supporting such an individual, they were slaughtering their own political interests. An association was made between black political interests and suppressing any black woman who desired to bring a black man down. According to Crenshaw, people incorrectly saw this as furthering their interests. Thus, in the case of Clarence Thomas, the black community shot itself in the foot. People found it more distressing that a black woman would say this man essentially discriminated against me in my job than it was distressing to say black civil rights leaders only moan and whine. To say that Thomas was whining about his treatment during the hearings, for example, would have been far more disturbing to African Americans. Yet this was the same man who referred to his sister as a belligerent, expectant, welfare dependant.[76]

Crenshaw was one of the black women law professors who supported Anita Hill at the hearings. "I looked at that situation and it really constituted for me a challenge for how I was going to continue to think about the collectivity called the black community. I mean, leaving that Senate every night, after having heard essentially white people attacking a black woman in a fairly traditional way, and then getting in a cab with the black cab driver who is also doing the same thing, and you go My God, you know, black women can be targeted both by white people and their own people. What must that mean?"[77]

Crenshaw believed that if the situation had been reversed—a black woman married to a white man, and a black man made these allegations— the African American community would have been much more indifferent, or even supportive of the man in question. Among more than a few black people, Crenshaw noted, gender is a distorting prism through which we see politics, and when this is coupled with the fact that color constitutes consciousness, you get a real, toxic form of race-conscious politics. Crenshaw argued that the Hill-Thomas hearings served as a permanent example about the need of the African American community to redefine the boundaries of political solidarity.

The long history of "not airing dirty linen," coupled with the fact that she brought unwanted attention to the black community, cost Anita Hill and her family. "My parents were exposed to ugliness in a way that was really unfair, and unfortunate, and hurtful to them," Hill said a year after the hearings in a televised interview. "I was publicly vilified . . . and that's something that I would not wish on anybody else." In spite of what she called a "reprehensible response" to her speaking out, Hill encouraged other women to come forward whenever they are victims of sexual harassment.[78]

In the three days over which the Judiciary Committee hearings took place, Clarence Thomas portrayed himself as a victim. During the hearings, he made his now well-known statement—that he was a victim of "a high-tech lynching for uppity blacks."[79] By evoking one of the most racially charged images possible, a black man being lynched, Thomas shrewdly and dramatically turned the hearings in his favor.[80] Whites and blacks were reminded of the not so distant past when black men swung from trees simply for being black, and especially when it was suspected they had violated the chastity and purity of a white woman.[81]

Thomas had always claimed, however, that racism had never been a problem for him and that he was, in fact, a self-made man. That Thomas would use the term lynching was both ironic and shameful on several levels. One ironic twist was that Thomas was not being accused by a white woman, but a black one. And the most visible irony of all, Crenshaw pointed out, was that his major support came from whites, such as Strom Thurmond, Senator John Danforth of Missouri, and Thomas's wife Virginia, who sat directly behind him.

Reaction to the three-day spectacle of the hearings and then the final vote was nothing short of incredible. Feminists adopted Hill as their new national "poster woman," and she was given numerous awards for her courage and daring, by *Glamour* and *Vanity Fair* magazines, for example, and by the organization 100 Black Women. While some black women's groups did not support Hill, the majority did.[82] She recounted the ambivalence that she encountered among some black women, as well as the gratitude she felt from many of them.

Shortly after the hearing, Jewel Jackson McCabe, founder of the coalition of 100 Black Women, a national civic and social organization made up of local chapters, invited me to New York to receive an award from the organization. Some of the local chapters agreed; others did not, reflecting the mixed feelings of the larger African American community. Nevertheless, I knew that only through Black women as individuals and as groups would I regain my place in the community. . . . Nevertheless, I knew there were African American women who fully appreciated my dilemma and embraced my right to speak as their own.[83]

Anita Hill became a darling in liberal and feminist circles and became a much sought-after speaker before women's groups and on college campuses. Hill, more often than not, rejected such invitations. In one of several books written about the hearings, two reporters stated: "Everyone wanted a piece of this woman. . . . There were people who thought she should be out there as a spokesman for women or whatever. Well, that is not what she wanted to do. That is not who she is. She did *not* want to be the Rosa Parks of sexual harassment."[84] As another book on the hearings put it, "Hovering around her were feminists who wanted to make sexual harassment the issue or diehard Thomas opponents who wanted to make him the issue. Hill's concern was simply that she had the opportunity to say what she wanted to do."[85] Yet, as Elsie Washington argues, "across the country, women began speaking out on and filing suits based on sexual harassment. Employers had to define sexual harassment and issue statements and memos about where their companies stood on the issue. The issue of sexual harassment in the workplace was forever etched into the nation's consciousness and linked forever with the three-day television 'seminar' in the U.S. Senate."[86]

Anita Hill described the effects of the hearings this way:

For weeks and months after the hearing of October 1991, professional news analysts and commentators attempted to explain the intense anger that erupted because of the proceedings. In retrospect it is difficult to understand how the various emotions intensified so rapidly during the confirmation hearing. In a relatively short time, anger, confusion, disappointment, distrust, and more anger reached a boiling point, as people around the country focused on their televisions or radios to try to comprehend the spectacle which the process became. The hearings combined a variety of potentially volatile elements—gender, race, power, sex, and yes, politics—which when combined and subjected to the glare of television caused a mild explosion.[87]

In addition, the Hill-Thomas hearings galvanized women into political action to change the face of an all-white, 98 percent male Senate. It is largely due to this fact that 1992 became a banner year for women in American politics. The November 1992 elections brought four more women to the Senate and twenty-four women to the House of Representatives. One new senator was Carol Mosley-Braun, an African American woman from Illinois, who had a large amount of support from women and African Americans in many states.[88] Mosley-Braun was the first African American woman to serve in the U.S. Senate. The media referred to 1992 as the Year of the Woman in Politics, and Anita Hill was given considerable credit for this.[89]

Because of the Hill-Thomas hearings, a number of black scholars called for more attention to be given to sexism in the black community. Black feminist intellectual extraordinaire bell hooks stated:

> Until black men can face the reality that sexism empowers them despite the impact of racism in their lives, it will be difficult to engage in meaningful dialogue about gender. Listening to black men talk about their social reality, one often hears narratives of victimization. Even very successful black men will talk about their lives as though racism is denying them access to forms of power they cannot even describe. . . . Historically the language used to describe the way black men are victimized within racist society has been sexualized. When words like castration, emasculation, and impotency are commonly used terms to describe the nature of black male suffering, a discursive practice is established that links black male liberation with gaining the right to participate fully within patriarchy. Embedded in this assumption is the idea that black women who are not willing to assist black men in their efforts to become patriarchs are 'the enemy.' . . . Until black women and men begin to seriously confront sexism in black communities, as well as within black individuals who live in predominantly white settings, we will continue to witness mounting tension and ongoing divisiveness between the two groups. Masculinity as it is conceived within patriarchy is life-threatening to black men.[90]

Although it seemed at first that Hill had been seen as the loser after the confirmation hearings, the fact is that she gave women of all races, and particularly black women, a voice, something they had often been denied.[91] A month after the hearings, a group of "1,603 women of African descent" (among them several of the women interviewed for this book) placed ads in major national newspapers stating, in part:

> We are particularly outraged by the racist and sexist treatment of Professor Anita Hill, an African American woman who was maligned and castigated for daring to speak publicly of her own experience of sexual abuse. The malicious defamation of Professor Hill insulted all women of African descent and sent a dangerous message to any woman who might contemplate a sexual harassment

complaint. . . . Many have erroneously portrayed the allegations against Clarence Thomas as an issue of either gender or race. As women of African descent, we understand sexual harassment as both. We further understand that Clarence Thomas outrageously manipulated the legacy of lynching in order to shelter himself from Anita Hill's allegations. To deflect attention away from the reality of sexual abuse in African American women's lives, he trivialized and misrepresented this painful part of African American people's history. This country, which has a long legacy of racism and sexism, has never taken the abuse of Black women seriously. Throughout U.S. history Black women have been sexually stereotyped as immoral, insatiable, perverse, the initiators in all sexual contacts—abusive or otherwise. The common assumption in legal proceedings as well as in the larger society has been that Black women cannot be raped or otherwise sexually abused. As Anita Hill's experience demonstrates, Black women who speak of these matters are not likely to be believed. . . . In 1991, we cannot tolerate this type of dismissal of any one Black woman's experience or this attack upon our collective character without protest, outrage, and resistance. . . . We pledge ourselves to continue to speak out in defense of one another, in defense of the African American community and against those who are hostile to social justice no matter what color they are. No one will speak for us but us.[92]

Though this statement was signed by a minute portion of the nation's black women, there is no doubt that many more would have signed it had they known about it.

On the Court, Thomas has voted in a manner that has pleased his conservative base. He has demonstrated himself to be a foe of unions, populism, affirmative action, and other progressive movements. Along with Justice Antonin Scalia, he is considered one of the Court's most conservative justices. Ironically Hill, although a Democrat, had a conservative bent, which was revealed in the landmark hearings, and in a CBS interview with the late legendary journalist Ed Bradley, she mentioned that she was a conservative Democrat.[93] Yet Hill's testimony before the Senate committee shone a spotlight on the progressive issue of gender equity. As one author argued, "She is credited with bringing attention to . . . a problem between men and women at work that had not, to that point, been perceived as a serious or necessarily addressable issue by men."[94]

In the years following the Hill-Thomas hearings, countless articles brought attention to the dilemmas facing single, well-educated, highly intelligent black women, the conflicts and obstacles that they face in regard to relationships, and the dating and marriage dilemmas they face. Many people argued that nothing was resolved at the end of the hearings. But many

Americans on both sides of the political aisle, including conservative columnist William Safire, noted that the hearings provided the opportunity for America to witness firsthand the black intelligentsia. According to Safire,

> Instead of seeing the usual parade of Black politicians or militant leaders demanding entitlements on television or seeing Blacks portrayed as humorous Cosbys or sitcom characters, the nation was exposed to an array of articulate, sincere, fiercely loyal (on both sides) witnesses from the upwardly mobile professional class. Long after we forget who was on which side, we will remember the intellectual sparkle of the history professor Nancy Fitch, and the moving testimony of Ellen Wells, the welfare manager. The cut-the-comedy summation of Carlton Stewart shut up senators Simpson and Leahy, and Stanley Grayson—who looked at first like a tackle for the New York Giants—turned out to be an incisive investment banker whose authoritarian presence contrasted with the bowl of quaking Jell-O that was the Senator from Alabama.[95]

This was a group up until this point that had been marginalized from the public eye. The Hill-Thomas hearings changed such previous obscurity.

In October 2007, more than sixteen years after the riveting hearings took place and captivated much of the nation, Clarence Thomas published his memoirs. Throughout his autobiography, he discussed Anita Hill several times. In almost every instance, he maintained his argument that Hill was a combative, largely incompetent, hypersensitive, aggressive, somewhat delusional individual with an undue interest in his private life and who often exaggerated her own abilities and self-worth:

> At some point near the end of 1982, Chris Roggerson, my chief of staff had filled me in on his interim performance evaluation of my personal staff. While most of the staffers had done well, Chris told me that Anita wasn't performing up to expectations and failed to finish her assignments on time. I hadn't realized that her work was so deficient, but I'd already noticed that she'd stopped coming to our morning meetings, evidently as the result of a quarrel with another staff member. Such quarrels were not uncommon—I'd also noticed Anita's rude attitude toward other members of my staff—and it had been bothering me as well that she seemed far too interested in my social calendar. She regularly inquired about my after-hours activities and on more than one occasion had asked if she could accompany me to my professional functions. Chris's unfavorable evaluation now caused her to become even more sullen and withdrawn.[96]

Thomas provides another account in which he attempts to convince the readers that Hill was obsessed with him. "I continued to hear from Anita Hill throughout this period, almost always when she wanted something. She called the office fairly regularly, usually speaking with Diane, and she also called me at my home on occasion until I changed my phone number."[97] An addendum, however, explains that Thomas changed his phone number not because of Hill, but because he had been receiving late night calls that disturbed his sleep. Later in his memoirs, he discussed what he saw as the disingenuously conceived image of Anita Hill that, according to him, had been fabricated by the mainstream media:

> On Sunday morning, courtesy of *Newsday*, I met for the first time an Anita Hill who bore little resemblance to the woman who had worked for me at EEOC and the Education Department. Somewhere along the line she had been transformed into a conservative, devoutly religious Reagan-administration employee. In fact she was a left-winger who'd never expressed any religious sentiments whatsoever during the time I'd known her, and the only reason why she'd held a job in the Reagan administration was because I'd given it to her. But truth was no longer relevant: keeping me off the Supreme Court was all that mattered. These pieces of her sordid tale only needed to hold up long enough to help her establish credibility with the public. They fell away as the rest of the story gained traction in the media, just as the fuel tank and booster rockets drop away from a space shuttle once it reaches the upper atmosphere.[98]

Thomas further argued:

> People who had worked with me at EEOC called by the score to say that they knew I'd done nothing to Anita Hill, and that the meek and humble young woman they'd seen on TV was nothing like the abrasive, ambitious person they had known. Some didn't even bother to call, but simply caught the next plane to Washington. Not all of them agreed with my political views, but every one of them was sure that Anita's story was a pure fabrication, and they were determined to right the wrong she'd done.[99]

It was evident that the allegations levied by Hill against Thomas in the fall of 1991 resulted in him becoming excessively embittered with her and the media in general. In a *New York Times* op-ed piece, Hill forcefully responded to what she saw as the latest round of smears by Thomas and his allies on the political right.

> In the portion of his book that addresses my role in the Senate hearings into his nomination, Justice Thomas offers a litany of unsubstantiated representations and outright smears that Republican senators made about me when I testified before the Judiciary Committee—that I was a "combative left-winger" who was "touchy" and prone to overreacting to slights. A number of independent authors have shown those attacks to be baseless. What's more,　their

reports draw on the experiences of others who were familiar with Mr. Thomas's behavior, and who came forward after the hearings. It's no longer my word against his.[100]

Throughout the article, Hill aggressively dismantled the various charges that were ascribed to her by Justice Thomas and concluded her piece by stating: "The question of whether Clarence Thomas belongs on the Supreme Court is no longer on the table—it was settled back in 1991. But questions remain about how we will resolve the kinds of issues my testimony exposed. My belief is that in the past 16 years we have come closer to making the resolution of these issues an honest search for the truth, which after all is at the core of all legal inquiry. My hope is that Justice Thomas's latest fusillade will not divert us from that path."[101] There is no question that both Anita Hill and Clarence Thomas are passionate individuals who both see the truth on their side. The debate among pro-Hill and pro-Thomas supporters will continue on for some time.

Anita Hill was not the only black law professor to become the target of politicians. Two years later, in the spring of 1993, another black female legal scholar, Lani Guinier, found herself in the center of a political controversy. The difference in this situation was that where Hill was a plaintiff of sorts, Guinier was the defendant. Moreover, in the case of Lani Guinier, her legal writings were challenged, and attacks on her took on a gendered tone. She was ridiculed for her "strange ideas," "strange hair," "strange name," but at least the intellectual capacity of African American women in particular, was acknowledged and given some power.[102] The Guinier controversy demonstrated that black women were not solely role models but also had the intellectual capacity, even if controversial, to serve as mentors as well.

As many Americans know, in early 1993 Lani Guinier, then a law professor at the University of Pennsylvania School of Law, was nominated by President Bill Clinton to be the administration's civil rights enforcement chief. The nomination was withdrawn several weeks later in the wake of a vicious opposition campaign from the political right that took by surprise a White House staff that was very green at the time. Conservatives started a malicious campaign against Guinier, in many cases distorting her legal writings.[103] Critics labeled her a "quota queen."[104] Some said she believed that virtually all government benefits, including elections, must be distributed along racial lines, and that white Americans remained implacably hostile to black progress.[105] She was alleged to have derided black Republicans and even some black Democrats, such as former Virginia governor Doug Wilder, as being only "descriptively" and not "authentically" black.[106] Each of these charges were false.[107] Conservative commentators had plucked sentences and even sentence fragments out of context, manipulating and distorting Guinier's writings in an effort to derail her nomination.

Guinier's supporters argued that her scholarly articles should certainly be examined and reviewed as part of a confirmation process, but that certain standards should also be met. For example, some legal scholars argued the selective passages should accurately reflect the nominee's overall views, and the writings in question should be relevant to the nominee's potential responsibilities.[108] As it turned out, such a level of fairness never presented itself in the Guinier nomination. Many reporters readily accepted conservative caricatures of her views.[109] The same convoluted misattributions resurfaced in mainstream publications such as *Newsweek*, the *Los Angeles Times*, and *U.S. News and World Report*. Instead of actually engaging in the responsible task of obtaining and reading her writings, much of the mainstream media was all too willing to substitute the tarnished code words that had been introduced by the conservative right—"quotas," "affirmative action," "reverse discrimination." Many made no effort to present Guinier's actual words. As legal scholar Laurel Leff argued: "There was no mention in any of these mainstream publications that Lani Guinier, in a number of law review articles, had explicitly rejected the use of electoral quotas and affirmative action remedies in voting rights cases."[110]

The vicious attacks on Guinier ignited a firestorm that the White House was unable to extinguish.[111] Her supporters were furious at the treatment that Guinier received and declared that she was being railroaded. As the controversy ensued, President Clinton made the decision to withdraw her nomination. Although the decision may have been unavoidable, it denied Guinier the hearing that nominees such as Zoe Baird, Robert Bork, and Clarence Thomas had when their nominations were thought to be in serious jeopardy.[112] Her critics saw it as the case of another black woman being marginalized, disrespected, and disregarded by a hostile white male power structure.[113]

The sort of treatment that Lani Guinier received was the beginning of a pattern that became commonplace by the 1990s. Instead of meticulously analyzing a nominee's record and scoring points by engaging in civil criticism, opponents tended to resort to ad hominem attacks, name calling, and hurling charges that in many cases were not only unsubstantiated but false. Washington politics had become a spectacle in which the side that shouted the loudest or appeared to be the most clever ended up victorious.[114]

For many reasons, this was an unfortunate turn of events, Yale University Law professor Stephen Carter argued. If Guinier had been granted the courtesy of a hearing, she would have had the chance to defend herself against critics' charges. A hearing would not have guaranteed confirmation but would have brought some level of fairness to what seemed a smear campaign and a witch hunt.[115] Her detractors would have been forced to provide a credible argument on why they perceived Guinier to be unfit to be assistant attorney general of the United States. Rather, we got a lot of heated rhetoric from both sides.[116]

The Guinier controversy was sparked by conservative activist Clint Bolick's *Wall Street Journal* article that criticized Guinier as an advocate of racial quotas when it comes to voting. "She demands equal legislative outcomes, requiring abandonment not only of the 'one person, one vote' principle, but majority rule itself."[117] The *Journal* chose the words "Clinton's Quota Queens" as the headline for the article, which was about two nominees, Guinier and a Latina. Soon afterward the article appeared, Bolick went on NPR's *Morning Edition* to denounce Guinier's writings: "Lani Guinier's writings are profoundly anti-democratic" and "amounted to a racial apartheid system."[118] From the outset, Guinier's enemies dominated the debate.[119]

After Bolick fired the opening shot, conservative columnist Paul Gigot referred to Guinier as "the reincarnation of John Calhoun."[120] Senator Bob Dole strongly attacked the nomination on the Senate floor and argued that "Guinier has been consistently hostile to the 'one person, one vote' principle, but majority rule itself."[121] Senator Alan Simpson accused Guinier of "reverse racism."[122] David Boldt, then editorial page editor of the *Philadelphia Inquirer*, denounced Guinier as a "madwoman" with "cockamamie ideas,"[123] and syndicated columnist George Will wrote that "Guinier favors federal imposition on state and local governments of rules that would generate results pleasing to groups she prefers."[124]

In her book *Lift Every Voice*, Guinier reflected on how she had been defined: "though 'quota queens' was coined in the plural the day after formal nomination, the term was quickly used to target me alone. After all, as a law professor, I was the only one with a paper trail."[125] Hardly any media outlet bothered to examine the motives of the conservative right or what Clint Bolick's agenda was. Bolick had a score to settle. As Guinier wrote:

> Interviewed in the *New York Times*, Bolick said, "Clinton has not had to expend any political capital on the issue of quotas and with her [Guinier] we believe we could inflict a heavy political cost." Clint Bolick had been a political appointee in the Reagan administration; he had helped draft many of the policies I criticized. Bolick was rarely identified as having a personal ax to grind; even Nina Totenberg, in an otherwise evenhanded piece on National Public Radio, quoted Bolick as if he were simply an informed critic, not an ideologue supported primarily by right-wing organizations like the Lynde and Harry Bradley Foundation.[126]

Apprehension about her nomination was not limited to conservatives. Yale Law Professor Stephen Carter, in his foreword to *The Tyranny of the Majority*, a collection of the legal writings of Lani Guinier, mentions that many moderates and even some liberals were concerned that Guinier's nomination or possible confirmation would result in a fragmented Democratic Party. Some argued that if confirmed, Guinier would raise the ire of conservative Democrats, and thus result in a balkanization of the party. Thomas Mann of the Brookings Institute feared a "polarization" that would make racial accommodation "virtually impossible." Even some traditional allies of the African American community were reluctant to support Guinier. The *New York Times* stated its wariness of Guinier. Liberal senators such as Diane Feinstein, Barbara Boxer, Carol Mosley Braun (at the time the only black person in the Senate), and Edward Kennedy declined to openly declare their support for Guinier. When asked why she had not come to the defense of Guinier, Carol Mosley Braun responded: "she has not asked me to do so."[127]

The media reported the charges about Guinier as if they were facts. Indeed, many reporters decided to report the arguments her opponents waged and speculated that those who supported Guinier would do so despite what they knew to be true about her writings. Laurel Leff wrote an excellent account of this sort of speculative, irresponsible journalism in an issue of the *Columbia Journalism Review*. According to Leff, "The fact that more than a few people in the media would fail to read her writings demonstrated the lack of consciousness and respect they had toward both the nomination and the nominee. Many were either too lazy, too dishonest, too incompetent or all three."[128]

Guinier's supporters included the NAACP and its then president, Ben Chavis, who denounced the treatment of Guinier by her critics as "reactionary." Liberal Vermont Senator Patrick Leahy stated on radio that Guinier "was tried in the press." Others referred to her treatment as vituperative. Even some of her opponents believed that she was treated unfairly. William Bennett later remarked, "I think she was given a very raw deal." Former president Gerald Ford stated, in reference to the collection of her writings, "I applaud the book, even though I disagree with many of its conclusions. It provides, in fairness, a forum for rebuttal that the White House, the Congress, and the news media denied."[129] Stephen Carter also made the point that although he did not agree with all of her writings, he concurred with Guinier supporters that her words in virtually every instance were "taken out of context or distorted." He further argued that many of Guinier's critics misunderstood her because they "failed to meet her at starting point: that votes should matter."[130]

In his book *The Confirmation Mess: Cleaning Up the Federal Appointments Process*, Carter provides a nuanced position about the treatment of Lani Guinier:

> Lani Guinier, not to put too fine a point on it, was railroaded. I do not mean that her opponents were not, for the most part, sincere individuals who thought that by derailing her nomination, they were somehow advancing the cause of racial justice. I mean, rather, that once her objectionable remarks are placed in their context—and once she is granted the freedom to experiment and imagine that scholarship demands—virtually all the critiques of her candidacy, and those that remain do not seem so serious that they should be used to deny confirmation, specially when one considers certain comparisons that will become obvious.[131]

Indeed, in the Guinier nomination, no one seemed to bother to see if her writings were in the mainstream or not. As far as they were concerned, she was "out of the mainstream" and thus problematic for President Clinton and the nation. The nomination was doomed.[132]

Guinier spoke of the polarization that her nomination caused: "That I did quickly become a lightning rod for controversy should not have been surprising. After all, I was talking about rebuilding a commitment to civil rights through innovative approaches in a climate in which much of the constituency for civil rights had been in hiding, in response to the systematic attacks of the past twelve years. The civil rights community had experienced the twelve years of Reagan/Bush Republican administrations as devastating."[133]

Much of the coverage of the nomination, whether intentionally or not, was racist, sexist, elitist, and xenophobic. As was the case with Anita Hill, a number of conservative and neoconservative magazines ran exaggerated pictures of Guinier on their covers.[134] To say the least, many of these images were demeaning. Guinier expressed her frustration and displeasure:

> Fueled by cartoonish caricatures provided by right-wing advocates the media soon defined me. I kept waiting for the White House to put together a strategy; meanwhile, the right wing had the field to itself. They succeeded in telling their story using my name and most important, my image. I was pigeonholed in a litany of alliteration. "Looney Lani," the "Czarina of Czeparatism," the "Princess of Proportionality," Clinton's "Quota Queen"—was a grotesque caricature of a stereotype. Quota Queen conflated three racialized images: welfare, quotas and unmarried, loud, demanding black women. . . . The right-wing story was that I wanted more for blacks, less for whites—apparently "by any means

necessary," including the destruction of democracy. "Quota Queen" made any further communication superfluous; it announced my agenda loud and clear: An imperious black woman who did not know her place, I would do to whites what centuries of whites had done to blacks. . . . I became Reagan's welfare queen tooling around the neighborhood in her Cadillac, mocking the hard work of others and the hard labor undertaken to produce this democratic system.[135]

What was most troubling to Guinier and many of her supporters was that the White House made no credible effort to defend the nomination when she was under a vicious assault by the right wing. Rather than refuting unsubstantiated charges, the White House declared they would not comment on a nominee while the candidate was in the nominating process. This allowed Guinier's opponents to viciously defame her. As the weeks progressed, the attacks became so brutal that Guinier thought the White House would break their silence. The fact that they did not refueled her frustration.

It was a month of laissez-faire treatment by the White House. Even if they were not worried, I was. I was particularly troubled by their absence of visible support." As the weeks passed, this frustration began to speak to her family members and relatives as well. "My mother worried as any mother would; she became increasingly agitated by the hostile press coverage and the absence of a serious White House response."[136]

In the liberal *Village Voice*, Columbia University law professor Patricia Williams provided a very astute analysis of the Guinier nomination: "For those familiar with her work this [began] to resemble some drunken party game in which each person gossips a message to his neighbor, each embroidering 'the story' until no story is left, only inebriated malice. As if that weren't enough, the most corrupt part is that the message that began all the whispering was not Lani Guinier's but Clint Bolick's."[137] The cluelessness and ignorance that Williams described was supported by the absence of several factors. The White House was inactive when it could have been recruiting political scientists, legal academics, and other political leaders to speak out on behalf of Guinier Laurel Leff argued. Given the dearth of politically progressive opinion makers who write about the experiences of women and people of color, and a tendency to promote neoconservative rhetoric, the messages of a few conservative and neoconservative writers enjoyed enormous circulation throughout various conservative think tanks, newspapers, electronic media, and other conservative venues.[138]

The Clinton administration argued initially that Guinier's law review articles should not be reported as the main focus of her nomination. Instead of taking this line of advice, the press ignored it, and the president, perhaps in frustration, abandoned this argument.[139] Only one major newspaper, the *Chicago Tribune*, suggested that the focus of the story might have been misdirected. Despite being critical of some of the opinions she had written in law review articles, the *Tribune* endorsed Guinier's nomination. "The error here—as in the case of Bork—is to assume what a scholar suggests in an academic article shows what she will pursue in public office. . . . No one is about to give the civil rights division the green light to try and get a court to demand a minority veto on legislation. Guinier, even if she were inclined, will not be allowed to push any radical agenda in litigation."[140]

Despite the unrelentingly hostile press coverage and the absence of a serious White House response, Guinier was asked to remain silent as a courtesy to the Senate while she awaited her confirmation hearings. Shortly before her nomination was withdrawn, Guinier recounted the tense conversation she had with Ricki Seidman, a Clinton staff official:

> "Well Ricki, I can't play out the political game with you. That is not my area of expertise. But people who I have confidence in have told me that if I testify, they think I will be confirmed. And I think even if I am not confirmed that I should at least be given an opportunity to testify and then if you want to revisit this after my hearing and you tell me that despite every best effort I can't be confirmed, that is a different story. But I am not going to withdraw." "Won't you even consider it?" she asked. "No," I said. "I will not withdraw." "You know, Lani," she said, "I think that maybe some of these people are right that you are not a team player and you weren't the right person for this job."[141]

Guinier found that Seidman's remarks emboldened her. She saw a hearing as a long-awaited opportunity that would give her a chance to respond to false charges. A hearing could invite the American people into a public conversation on the racial justice issues at the core of her writing. She also felt that the White House—by not coming to her defense, insisting that she remain silent, and then advocating that she withdraw her nomination—was failing to honor basic fundamental principles of fairness that were essential to the democratic process. "I believed that everything the Democratic Party and that this president stood for was reflected in my position. By fighting for a hearing I was pushing the administration to do what it was not then prepared to do—fight for principles of fairness now, and in the long term show its commitment to put social justice issues front and center before the American people."[142]

Yale Law Professor Stephen Carter described the "confirmation angst" that attended the Guinier saga and says that the fact she never got a hearing is a "terrible shame." According to Carter, "there was actually something to be accomplished by holding hearings." As he points out, "had her accusers been forced to raise their charges in a forum in which Guinier herself was entitled to equal time—the hearing room—we might have had the televised 'national seminar' that some have said we got in the Bork hearings, this time on the fundamental dilemma that has shaped our nation's history: the dilemma of race."[143]

There is no doubt that the savage treatment of Guinier, the harrowing nomination process, and the media firestorm that erupted could have been averted. Instead of taking statements as "facts" from Clint Bolick, the *Wall Street Journal*, and various conservative publications, reporters could have read some of Guinier's law review articles, or they could have adhered to the message by the Clinton White House to not make Guinier's legal writings the focus of so much attention. Moreover, the administration could have undertaken a more aggressive defense of the nominee and forcefully demanded that she be granted the courtesy of a hearing.[144] Guinier might not have been confirmed, but we all would have benefited had the president insisted on going forward with the hearings and the Senate Judiciary Committee had conducted a "national seminar" on the issues at the core of the controversy.

Former President Bill Clinton, in his autobiography *My Life*, described how he saw the events of the spring of 1993:

> June began with a disappointment that was both personal and political, as I withdrew my nomination of Lani Guinier, a University of Pennsylvania professor, a longtime lawyer for the NAACP Legal Defense Fund, and my law school classmate, to be the career civil rights lawyer to head the Civil Rights Division. After I named her in April, the conservatives went after Guinier with a vengeance, attacking her as a "quota queen" and accusing her of advocating the abandonment of the constitutional principle of "one man, one vote" because she had supported a system of cumulative voting under which each voter would get as many votes as there are contested seats on a legislative body, and could cast all the votes for a single candidate. In theory, cumulative voting could dramatically increase the odds of minority candidates being elected.[145]

Clinton further stated: "At first I did not pay too much attention to the rantings of the right, thinking that what they really disliked about Guinier was her long record of successful civil rights fights, and that as she made the rounds of the Senate, she would win enough votes to be confirmed easily." Clinton stated that he found her law review articles somewhat persuasive but ultimately in opposition to what he considered proper support for affirmative action and his resistance to quotas, and they seemed to advocate a "one man, many votes" philosophy.[146] This argument was fully discredited by legal scholar Stephen Carter, however, who says Guinier was stating that votes should count.

Clinton concluded his discussion of Lani Guinier by stating: "In the aftermath, I was heavily criticized for abandoning a friend in the face of political pressure, mostly by people who didn't know what was going on in the background. Eventually, I nominated Deval Patrick, another brilliant African American lawyer with a strong civil rights background, to lead the Civil Rights Division, and he did a fine job. I still admire Lani Guinier, and regret that I lost her friendship."[147] Ultimately, Clinton's discussion of the Guinier controversy is brief and somewhat dismissive.

A number of people argue that Lani Guinier was "borked," referring to Supreme Court nominee Robert Bork, whose nomination in 1987 by President Ronald Reagan failed after numerous charges were hurled against him that he was too far out of the mainstream. This comparison, while not entirely accurate, could be seen as a relatively reasonable analogy. Yet, unlike Lani Guinier, Judge Bork was condemned by his own words, not the words that others appended to him. Bork, in other words, had a hearing.

Anita Hill and Lani Guinier, two black female legal scholars, found themselves thrust into the center of two nationally gripping controversies. One was a plaintiff of sorts, fighting an uphill battle to tell her story to an all-white, all-male, generally hostile Judiciary Committee, a largely embarrassed African American public, and a small core of feminist supporters and other liberals. The other was in the position of defendant, who was required to remain silent while others launched reckless ad hominem attacks, called her names, and lobbed false charges of radical extremism.[148] This was how many journalists and legal scholars who covered the two events summed it up. Both were unsuccessful in their initial efforts. However, as time progressed, they used their public platforms to engage in a long-term dialogue about the issues at stake. Their missions eventually succeeded in that they were able to bring serious issues such as race, gender, sexual harassment, the structure of political opportunity, and reapportionment, among others, to the forefront of discussion in American society.

The Hill and Guinier cases display the feelings, isolation, marginalization, disrespect, and hostile treatment that these two very successful, intelligent, African American legal scholars endured at the hands of a largely hostile or indifferent public and media. Anita Hill and Lani Guinier, while better known to the public than most black women legal scholars due to their presence in the media spotlight, have contemporaries who have similar stories of isolation, marginalization, hostile work environments, racism, sexism, elitism, and other vices that have been a part of their experiences. We will see these stories unfold in future chapters.

Notes

1. Neil Lewis, "Law Professor Accuses Thomas of Sexual Harassment in the 1980s," *New York Times*, October 6, 1991, A1, A14. Various news media outlets, both print and cable, covered the Clarence Thomas and Anita Hill hearings at length.

2. A number of journalists were spellbound by the hearings. Nina Totenberg, who at the time worked for National Public Radio, was the journalist who broke the story.

3. Elsie Washington, *Uncivil War: The Struggle between Black Men and Women* (Chicago: Noble, 1996).

4. Telephone interview with Taunya Lovell Banks, January 24, 2006.

5. *Roe v. Wade*, 419 U.S. (1973).

6. Nomination of Judge Clarence Thomas to be Associate Justice of the Supreme Court of the United States, Hearings before the Committee on the Judiciary, U.S. Senate, 102nd Cong, 1st Sess., October 12, 1991.

7. Washington, *Uncivil War*, 50.

8. Anita Hill, *Speaking Truth to Power* (New York: Doubleday, 1997), 4–5.

9. Hill, *Speaking Truth to Power*.

10. The black community was deeply divided on the Hill-Thomas hearings. Many blacks were upset that the divisions that had long existed in private between black men and women were finally being aired in public for the larger community to see.

11. Washington, *Uncivil War*, 51–56.

12. Washington, *Uncivil War*, 50.

13. During the Hill-Thomas hearings, a number of African Americans called radio talk shows and television programs expressing their dismay at the situation that was taking place.

14. Washington, *Uncivil War*, 50.

15. Washington, *Uncivil War*, 51–60. There was a plethora of commentary from diverse segments of the black community arguing this fact.

16. Throughout much of our history, and even today in some quarters, frank and open discussion about sexuality among black women is considered taboo and off limits.

17. Washington, *Uncivil War*, 51.

18. Washington, *Uncivil War*, 51.

19. Kimberlé Crenshaw, "Whose Story Is It Anyway? Feminist and Antiracist Appropriations of Anita Hill," in *Race-ing, Justice, En-gendering Power: Essays on Anita Hill, Clarence Thomas, and the Construction of Social Reality*, ed. Toni Morrison (New York: Pantheon, 1992), 406.

20. Washington, *Uncivil War*, 51–52.

21. Stephanie M. Wildman and Trina Grillo, *Privilege Revealed: How Invisible Preference Undermines America* (New York: New York University Press, 1996), 67–84.

22. Washington, *Uncivil War*, 53.

23. By the mid-1990s, several years after the hearings had taken place, polls demonstrated that the majority of public sentiment had shifted in favor of Anita Hill.

24. Washington, *Uncivil War*, 53–54. This certainly was the sentiment among many black Americans.

25. Washington, *Uncivil War*, 54.

26. Numerous literary works and historical documents have reported the plight that many black men have endured at the hands of a hostile white society.

27. By the late 1960s, a number of women, including more than a few black women, began to challenge male domination and patriarchy. This new resistance among women resulted in some resentment among men, including black men.

28. Washington, *Uncivil War*, 34.

29. Washington, *Uncivil War*, 52.

30. Nell Painter, "Hill, Thomas, and the Use of Racial Stereotype," in Morrison, *Race-ing, Justice, En-gendering Power*, 200–214.

31. Painter, "Hill, Thomas, and the Use of Racial Stereotype."

32. Washington, *Uncivil War*, 53. This is the belief of a considerable number of black men and women.

33. In the early to mid-1990s, a number of articles written by black men confirmed this concern. Monroe, "Sex, Lies, and Stereotype"; Earl Ofari Hutchinson, "No Thriller Superstar for Michael Jackson," *Emerge Magazine*, March 1994, 64; Marc A. Cummings, "Politics, Black Women, and Easy Prey," *Emerge Magazine*, December–January 1995, 84; Kevin A. Ross, "The Bogeyman Still Haunts Many White Minds," *Emerge Magazine*, February 1995, 84.

34. Mary A. Fischer, "The Witch Hunt," *Gentleman's Quarterly*, December 1993.

35. Monroe, "Sex, Lies, and Stereotype."

36. Washington, *Uncivil War*, 54.

37. Washington, *Uncivil War*.

38. Hill, *Speaking Truth to Power*, 274.

39. Jill Mary and Jill Abramson, *Strange Justice: The Selling of Clarence Thomas* (New York: Plume, 1995), 249.

40. Nomination of Judge Clarence Thomas, Hearings before the Committee on the Judiciary, October 14, 1991.

41. Nomination of Judge Clarence Thomas, Hearings before the Committee on the Judiciary, October 12, 1991.

42. Anita Hill and Emma Coleman-Jordan, *Race, Gender, and Power in America: The Legacy of the Hill-Thomas Hearings* (New York: Oxford University Press), 148.

43. "Public Hearing, Private Pain," *Frontline*, PBS, October 13, 1992; Washington, *Uncivil War*, 54.

44. Nellie McKay, "Remembering Anita Hill and Clarence Thomas: What Really Happened When One Black Woman Spoke Out," in Morrison, *Race-ing, Justice, En-gendering Power*, 285.

45. Hill, *Speaking Truth to Power*, 179–86, 190–93, 194–95.

46. Hill and Coleman-Jordan, *Race, Gender, and Power in America*, 273.

47. Dickerson, "Why Is Anita Hill Out to Get Judge Thomas?" *Atlanta Constitution*, October 11, 1991. Janet Cooke, a *Washington Post* journalist, won the Pulitzer Prize for her news article "Jimmy's World," but it was later revealed that she had invented parts of the story. Tawana Brawley, a teenager from upstate New York, accused law enforcement officers of a grotesque and racially motivated sexual assault and abduction, but the case later turned out to be a hoax.

48. Anita Hill, "Marriage and Patronage in the Empowerment and Disempowerment of African American Women," in Hill and Coleman-Jordan, *Race, Gender, and Power in America*, 275.

49. Hill, "Marriage and Patronage," 209.

50. Washington, *Uncivil War*, 54.

51. Mayer and Abramson, *Strange Justice*, 249.

52. Mayer and Abramson, *Strange Justice*, 249.

53. Mayer and Abramson, *Strange Justice*, 249.

54. Wildman and Grillo, *Privilege Revealed*, 82–83.

55. Washington, *Uncivil War*, 54.

56. Orlando Patterson, "Race, Gender, and Liberal Fallacies," *New York Times*, op-ed page, October 20, 1991.

57. Washington, *Uncivil War*, 54–55. Several of the women law professors that I interviewed recited stories of sexual misconduct from men at some point in their lives.

58. A number of black women's magazines, among them *Essence*, printed stories where black women recounted being the victims of unwanted sexual harassment from men.

59. Washington, *Uncivil War*, 55. Interview with Kimberlé Crenshaw, March 11, 1999.

60. Washington, *Uncivil War*, 55–60.

61. Adrienne M. Davis and Stephanie Wildman, "The Legacy of Doubt: Treatment of Sex and Race in the Hill-Thomas Hearings," *Southern California Law Review* 65 (1992); *Designing Women*, "The Strange Case of Clarence and Anita," CBS Television Broadcast, November 4, 1991; Wildman and Grillo, *Privilege Revealed*, 78–83.

62. Davis and Wildman, *The Legacy of Doubt*; Wildman and Grillo, *Privilege Revealed*.

63. Hill, *Speaking Truth to Power*, 127.

64. Hill, *Speaking Truth to Power*, 154.

65. Anita Hill interview by Jill Nelson, "Anita Hill: No Regrets," *Essence*, March 1992.

66. Hill, *Speaking Truth to Power*, 249–50.

67. A number of newspapers and magazines, among them *USA Today*, the *New York Times*, and *Ebony*, have lamented the dearth of black men compared with black women in our nation's largest cities. Washington, *Uncivil War*, 56.

68. Washington, *Uncivil War*.

69. Virginia Lamp Thomas, "Breaking Silence," *People*, November 11, 1991, 111.

70. Hill, *Speaking Truth to Power*, 342.

71. David Brock, "The Real Anita Hill," *American Spectator*, March 1992, 18–30. Brock followed up with a book-length work, *The Real Anita Hill* (New York: Free Press, 1994).

72. Hill, *Speaking Truth to Power*, 282.

73. David Brock, *Blinded by the Right: The Conscience of an Ex-Conservative* (New York: Crown, 2002).

74. Crenshaw interview, March 11, 1999.

75. Crenshaw interview, March 11, 1999.

76. Crenshaw interview, March 11, 1999. Accounts of Thomas's disrespectful manner toward his sister appeared in a number of publications.

77. Crenshaw interview, March 11, 1999.

78. In both print and electronic media, Anita Hill encouraged women who had been the victims of sexual harassment to come forward and expose their harassers as opposed to suffering in silence.

79. Nomination of Judge Clarence Thomas, Hearings before the Committee on the Judiciary, October 14, 1991.

80. A number of commentators, liberal and conservative, argued that Clarence Thomas was brilliant in his use of the term "high-tech lynching." This term, many believed, put the Senate Judiciary Committee on the defensive and provided him the ammunition he needed to secure a seat on the Supreme Court.

81. Crenshaw interview, March 11, 1999.

82. Washington, *Uncivil War*, 55–61.

83. Hill, *Speaking Truth to Power*, 275.

84. Timothy Phelps and Helen Winternitz, *Capitol Games: The Inside Story of Clarence Thomas and Anita Hill and a Supreme Court Nomination* (New York: Perennial), 1993.

85. Stephen Carter, *The Confirmation Mess: Cleaning Up the Federal Appointments Process* (New York: Basic Books), 1994.

86. Washington, *Uncivil War*, 55–61.

87. Hill, *Speaking Truth to Power*, 124.

88. Washington, *Uncivil War*, 58.

89. Many publications credited 1992 as a banner year for woman politicians due to the fact that many women were successful in getting elected to public office, including the U.S. Senate.

90. bell hooks, *Yearning: Race, Gender, and Cultural Politics* (Boston: South End, 1990), 57–58.

91. Washington, *Uncivil War*, 59.

92. In the fall of 1991, more than 300 prominent black women signed their names to a document that appeared in the *New York Times*. This ad eventually resulted in the organization Black Women in Defense of Ourselves.

93. Anita Hill, interview by Ed Bradley, *60 Minutes*, CBS, February 16, 1992.

94. Washington, *Uncivil War*, 61.

95. William Safire, "Myths of the Confirmation," *New York Times*, October 17, 1991, A27.

96. Clarence Thomas, *My Grandfather's Son: A Memoir* (New York: Harper-Collins, 2007), 171.

97. Thomas, *My Grandfather's Son*, 179.

98. Thomas, *My Grandfather's Son*.

99. Thomas, *My Grandfather's Son*.

100. Anita Hill, "The Smear This Time," *New York Times*, October 2, 2007, A25.

101. Hill, "The Smear This Time."

102. Patricia Williams, "Lani! We Hardly Knew Ye! How the Right Wing Created a Monster out of a Civil Rights Advocate and Bill Clinton Ran in Terror," *Village Voice*, June 15, 1993.

103. A number of conservative organizations and media outlets, among them the Heritage Foundation, *Washington Times*, *American Spectator*, *National Review*, *Wall Street Journal*, and Institute for Justice, engaged in a vicious character assassination and what many could argue was a dishonest campaign against Lani Guinier.

104. Clint Bolick, "Clinton's Quota Queens," *Wall Street Journal*, April 30, 1993.

105. Paul Gigot, "Hillary's Choice on Civil Rights: Back to the Future," *Wall Street Journal*, May 7, 1993.

106. Stuart Taylor Jr., "DOJ Nominee's Authentic Black Views," *Legal Times*, May 17, 1993.

107. Laurel Leff, "From Legal Scholar to Quota Queen: What Happens When Politics Pulls the Press into the Groves of Academe," *Columbia Journalism Review*, 32:3 (1993): 39.

108. Leff, "From Legal Scholar to Quota Queen," 37–41.

109. A number of "mainstream" and even a few left-leaning publications willingly bought into the rhetoric that was being trumpeted by large segments of the conservative right.

110. Leff, "From Legal Scholar to Quota Queen."

111. Lani Guinier, *Lift Every Voice: Turning a Civil Rights Setback into a New Vision of Social Justice* (New York: Simon and Schuster, 1998).

112. Lani Guinier, *The Tyranny of the Majority: Fundamental Fairness in Representative Democracy* (New York: Free Press, 1994), foreword by Stephen Carter, viii, ix.

113. A number of commentators, journalists, and even some politicians, both Democrats and Republicans, decried what they saw as the shameful behavior that Lani Guinier received during the confirmation hearings.

114. Leff, "From Legal Scholar to Quota Queen," 38–41.

115. Leff, "From Legal Scholar to Quota Queen," 38–41; Carter, in Guinier, *The Tyranny of the Majority*, xii–xv.

116. Leff, "From Legal Scholar to Quota Queen," 38–41; Carter, in Guinier, *The Tyranny of the Majority*, xii–xv.

117. Bolick, "Clinton's Quota Queens."

118. During the Lani Guinier confirmation hearings, Clint Bolick, Paul Gigot of the *Wall Street Journal*, and a number of conservative commentators took to the airwaves and denounced Guinier's writings as "radical," "undemocratic," and a "threat to democracy." Such activity took place for several weeks.

119. Carter, in Guinier, *The Tyranny of the Majority*.

120. Guinier, *The Tyranny of the Majority*, 134.

121. Guinier, *Lift Every Voice*, 48.

122. Guinier, *The Tyranny of the Majority*, 154.

123. David Boldt, "Guinier's Writings Would Have Hurt Her," *Philadelphia Inquirer*, June 6, 1993.

124. Carter, in Guinier, *The Tyranny of the Majority*, viii, ix.

125. Guinier, *Lift Every Voice*, 37.

126. Guinier, *Lift Every Voice*, 38.

127. Carter, in Guinier, *The Tyranny of the Majority*, viii, ix. Carol Mosley Braun, former U.S. Senator from Illinois, was quoted by several mainstream newspapers, including the *Washington Post*, *New York Times*, and *Los Angeles Times*.

128. Leff, "From Legal Scholar to Quota Queen," 38–41.

129. Carter, in Guinier, *The Tyranny of the Majority*, xi. Gerald R. Ford provided his comments in endorsing Guinier's collection of writings.

130. Carter, in Guinier, *The Tyranny of the Majority*, vii–xx.

131. Carter, *The Confirmation Mess*, 38.

132. Leff, "From Legal Scholar to Quota Queen," 37–41.

133. Guinier, *Lift Every Voice*, 32.

134. This was certainly true in the case of conservative magazines such as the American Spectator.

135. Guinier, *Lift Every Voice*, 37.

136. Guinier, *Lift Every Voice*.

137. Williams, "Lani! We Hardly Knew Ye!" 25–28.

138. Leff, "From Legal Scholar to Quota Queen," 38–41; Carter, in Guinier, *The Tyranny of the Majority*, xii–xv.

139. Leff, "From Legal Scholar to Quota Queen," 41.

140. *Chicago Tribune*, May 27, 1993, op-ed page.

141. Guinier, *Lift Every Voice*, 111.

142. Guinier, *Lift Every Voice*, 109–13.

143. Carter, in Guinier, *The Tyranny of the Majority*, viii.

144. Williams, "Lani! We Hardly Knew Ye!" 25–28.

145. Bill Clinton, *My Life* (New York: Knopf, 2004), 524.

146. Clinton, *My Life*, 523.

147. Clinton, *My Life*, 524.

148. Washington, *Uncivil War*, 49.

CHAPTER TWO

~

A Hostile and
Unsupportive Environment

The United States did not see a significant number of black faculty members entering the academy until the mid-1960s, or a significant number of women, including black women, until the 1970s. In 1971, Joyce Anne Hughes became the first black woman tenure-track law professor at a predominantly white school. At the time, Hughes was unaware of the history that would locate her along a continuum of previous black women who taught law in American colleges or in their own law offices.[1] Lutie A. Lytle, also African American, became America's first woman law professor in 1897, teaching in a black law school at Central Tennessee College.[2] Sybil Jones Dedmond, the first African American woman tenure-track law professor, taught from 1951 to 1964 at an ABA-approved black law school at North Carolina Central.[3]

While Dedmond's students were all African American and predominantly male due to the mores, laws, and customs of the segregated South, Hughes's students were mostly upper-class, well-schooled white males who had been socialized in predominantly white, conservative environments. Because of this dynamic, Dedmond had no problem earning the respect of her students; many of these young black men had been primarily taught by black women most of their lives.[4] Hughes's students, for the most part, had little, if any interaction with black people, let alone a black woman legal scholar. In another first, Hughes was the first black woman graduate of the University of Minnesota Law School, where she began her career. Hughes was also the first woman of any race to become a full-time faculty member at the institution.[5]

Because Hughes was both, black and female, she suffered the double jeopardy of racism and sexism.[6] That double jeopardy still exists. In 1994, women were 26 percent of full-time law professors,[7] but only 177 were black women.[8] Thus, black women were only 3.5 percent of all law professors.

Needless to say, when Hughes was hired as a law professor, her appointment received some media attention.[9] Overlooking its significance in black history, the *Minneapolis Star* referred to her appointment as "a gain for women's lib."[10] Her selection, however, did not sit well with some black students at the institution, particularly some black males who, it was rumored, would have "preferred a black man on the faculty."[11] In the year Hughes began her career as a law professor, women comprised about 9 percent of total law school enrollment; about half were first-year students.[12] Black enrollment was 50 percent of this figure. In all ABA-approved schools in 1971–1972, blacks were 4.1 percent of all students, and almost half were in their first year.[13] There are no exact statistics that provide how many female or black students there were. The number was undoubtedly small, if judged by the number of African American women lawyers and judges in 1970—only 500.[14]

Although black women law professors confront the double jeopardy of being both black and female, many of the dilemmas they endure are duplicative of those experienced by black male professors and women professors.[15] When Hughes faced a hearing in her second year of teaching, the minority groups section of the Association of American Law Schools (AALS) composed a list of expectations that they had of Hughes:

> to be a counselor to individual black and other minority students, as well as a tutor, a friend, a companion and a champion; to be a recruiter for black and other minority group students and for women students; to be available for unscheduled consultation on the "black question" or the "woman question"; to participate in formal and informal seminars on race relations and sex stereotyping; to endure with grace and tolerance both inadvertent and overt racial slurs; to serve on all special committees relating to minority groups and women; and, of course, to teach her regular classes, serve on the regular faculty committees, publish scholarly articles and be "one of the boys."[16]

According to Hughes, the June 1973 hearing was characterized by the dean as a special meeting of the University of Minnesota Law faculty. It ran nine and one-half hours long. Fourteen observers also attended all or part of the meeting, including representatives from the AALS, the Association of American University Professors (AAUP), the Minneapolis Urban League, and students.[17] Hughes recalled that she was seated at a table in front, with the dean, Carl Auerbach, who had replaced the dean in office when she was hired and had been her professor. A year after the special faculty meeting, he espoused negative statements about affirmation action which "greatly angered many law students."[18]

The genesis of the June 1973 meeting was a University of Minnesota Law School Grievance Committee handling of a student petition six months earlier, in December 1972. According to Hughes, the groundwork for this incident began in September 1972. She was teaching one of two sections of Legal Professions, a course dealing with lawyers' ethical responsibilities that was the only *required* third-year course.[19] At the beginning of the 1972–1973 academic year, students sought faculty approval to change the evaluation from the normal grading to a Pass/Fail system. A faculty committee recommended approval, and both Hughes and the professor teaching the other section remained neutral when the issue was brought to the full faculty. The faculty rejected the student request in September.[20] Hughes recounted that on a Friday in December, seven days before the scheduled exam, students requested that the faculty grant Pass/Fail grading in her section alone because of (a) her alleged excessive cancellation of classes or ill-timed make-up classes and/or (b) that she was unprepared to teach a course in Legal Professions. A "supplemental allegation" was added, complaining that students who had registered for the other section were assigned to hers.[21]

Although the matter of Pass/Fail grading for both sections had been decided at the beginning of the academic year, the faculty decided this was not a matter directed to Hughes individually and referred it to the Grievance Committee. The Monday after the student petition was presented to the Friday faculty meeting, the Grievance Committee met with some students, and because it found the petition "too vaguely drafted to serve as a fair basis for a hearing," it took oral statements from the students and rewrote the petition. Hughes mentioned that she received a copy two hours before the grievance committee hearing. The "supplemental allegation" mentioned above was added one hour before the hearing. At the hearing, the grievants presented their case and were cross-examined by Hughes and Joseph Hudson, the black male president of the Black American Law Students Association (BALSA). Hughes presented a defense. According to Hughes, the committee did not follow general rules of evidence or standard procedures for taking objections to testimony. This was both because the shortness of time seemed to call for less formal procedures to ensure fairness and because the committee viewed its function as conciliatory as well as adjudicative.[22]

The committee submitted its report to the faculty two days later. Its recommendation that the student petition for Pass/Fail grading be denied was adopted by the faculty, but the full report was not submitted for faculty action. That report said that the committee's "proceedings may have augmented the hostility already present in this matter." It also attempted to explain "why Professor Hughes was chosen for particular attention by the students" by noting that she was a second-year teacher, that the course Legal Professions was subjective, and that the Code of Professional Responsibility had recently been revised. Of the two sections of the course, only the first "explanation" applied to Hughes alone. The other two were equally applicable to the white male teaching the other section, but he was not singled out for "particular attention."[23] Hughes mentioned, "There were two other second-year teachers, persons younger than I but who had started teaching at the same time I did. Both were white males. Neither was subject to the outrageous treatment I endured."[24]

Hughes was incensed that the student petition was referred to the Grievance Committee. She firmly believed that the initial attempt to receive Pass/Fail grading undoubtedly occurred because she had started teaching a section of the Legal Professions course. No such attempt was made in prior years when both sections were taught by white males. According to Hughes, the faculty made its own decision to require the usual grading with no prodding from either her or the other professor.[25] If the faculty had chosen the Pass/Fail route for *both* sections, Hughes and the professor teaching the other section would have been treated equally. Hughes felt that the attempt to obtain Pass/Fail grading in her section alone indicated student unwillingness to have a black woman judge performance in a required course. What was most distressing to her, however, was that the faculty failed to treat a "colleague" with courtesy and lent support to student prejudices by referral to the Grievance Committee.[26]

Following the faculty's adoption of the recommendation of the committee, Hughes distributed a memo "to correct . . . an inadequate record of the events," and to express her "severe dissatisfaction with the faculty's method of handling the matter." Her memo made particular reference to the fact that it was not indicated anywhere "that the character or quality of teaching will be determined in an adversary setting, precipitated by a student petition."[27] Hughes discussed that during this time period, BALSA also distributed a memorandum to the faculty pointing out that the action was without precedent and that the hearing "denied Professor Hughes the type of courtesy usually given to a faculty member."[28] According to Hughes, there was no response by the faculty to her memo or to BALSA. In her conversations with the dean, he asserted that she had no complaint since she "prevailed" and no malice was intended. He encouraged Hughes to forget about the matter.[29]

The special faculty meeting of June 11, 1973, took place due to the fact that Hughes refused to forget what had transpired. The only motion adopted at that meeting extended an apology to her, but only for lack of adequate notice. According to Hughes, the majority of the meeting avoided discussion of the question of race and negative treatment. As the meeting concluded, the president of the Minneapolis Urban League stated that the black community had come to the conclusion that equal and fair treatment had been denied to Hughes. He labeled the hearing "a travesty of justice." In response to this situation, Hughes cynically replied, "But 'justice' was probably not a reasonable expectation from the same faculty which permitted the committee to act in a '75 percent adversary manner' on a student petition requesting Pass/Fail grading."[30]

Hughes adamantly argued that the petition lodged against her was not due to any lack of qualifications on her part. "When I started teaching, my credentials were as good as the white males on the faculty—and better than some." But those paper credentials did nothing to protect Hughes from hostile students, nor did they persuade the faculty and dean to treat her as a colleague who had equal qualifications. Rather, her colleagues chose to align with white students rather than a black professor. Nor was it about investing a course with racial perspectives. Rather, Hughes believed that the students were simply rejecting the idea of having a black woman pass judgment on their performance, particularly in a course that was essential to graduation, given that Legal Profession was a third-year required course.[31] Hughes's experience was not much different from that of numerous other black faculty who have argued that there is no presumption of competence for black professors as there is for whites. In fact, there is a presumption of incompetence. Simply being good at what one does generally will not be acknowledged for black law professors.

Hughes says that some colleagues and others had difficulty understanding her protest over the Grievance Committee matter, particularly since the committee denied the student petition for Pass/Fail grading.[32] She argued that to have remained silent would have been taken as acquiescence in the propriety of the Grievance Committee even addressing the issue.[33] "It is clear that they were dealing with the competency question since the faculty had previously rejected Pass/Fail grading for the course. Nonetheless, it was considered, assuming the complainant's allegations could be shown."[34] Hughes further argued that the Grievance Committee episode also underscored the importance of having an appropriate individual heading a law school.

William B. Lockhard, the dean at the time she was hired, served in the position from 1956 to 1972. Hughes believed that had he still been at the helm, the student petition issue would have been handled much more professionally.[35]

The year following the grievance matter, Hughes was considered for tenure. Rather than grant tenure, the decision was to renew her probationary appointment. In a letter to Hughes, the dean indicated that he and other faculty had come to the conclusion that Hughes did "not care to participate in [the] life" of the law school apart from her "classroom and special tutorial duties." The dean also stated that the faculty "are also most anxious to cultivate with you the same informal, warm spirit of free communication and true collegiality that the rest of the faculty enjoys."[36] Hughes responded to the dean that such a desire would have been welcome if it meant that one could retain viewpoints more reflective of the African American experience and maintain one's cultural identity as an African American woman. However, given the amount of cultural negation and assimilation that such a sacrifice would require, she would have no choice except to say no.[37] In short, Hughes's colleagues were telling her to "just be more like us, harbor no dissenting opinions, particularly on racial and gender issues," and everything will be just fine.

Hughes argued that to be the only African American, the only female, and the only black woman law teacher in an environment amplifies even additional pressure to conform to a white male norm. A critical mass of black persons facilitates individual blacks in that mass to retain their uniqueness. Although the numbers were small, there was a "mass" at Northwestern University School of Law when Hughes arrived in 1974 as a visiting professor, compared with the University of Minnesota Law School.[38] That was one factor in her acceptance of Northwestern's offer for her to join the regular faculty.[39]

Hughes and other black legal scholars argued that the mere presence of a black woman law professor can be instructive.[40] They argue that her presence brings that which majority students often obtain from majority professors— that African Americans and other minority students are capable and competent. In addition, simply seeing a black woman law professor means other blacks may consider it a career option.[41] Hughes made the case that *all* students, and the legal academy itself, deserve exposure to professors who are committed to truly educate—a word whose root means to "lead forth." Moreover, Hughes's experience suggests that the leadership of one person can draw out others from entrenched misconceptions.[42]

She believed that black women law professors can be in the vanguard of those who lead the legal academy forth from the erroneous belief that rationality implies "point-of-viewlessness."[43] Furthermore, she argued that black women professors can begin to develop a pedagogy that addresses the "intense alienation" of minority students whose "values, beliefs, and experiences clash not only with those of their classmates but also with those of their professors."[44] Such a pedagogy may in fact be beneficial to all students.[45]

Hughes believed that while each black woman law professor must develop her own method to cope with the demands of the academy, they all can and should be uniquely who they are—black women—and bring that to bear on what they do—teach law. She feels often it is believed that people are what they do. To the extent that teaching law is equated with being a white male (or even a white female), then black women law professors must insist on the dichotomy between who they are and what they do—a distinction she argued she has tried to maintain even in the beginning.[46] "Because the past is with us in the present," Hughes stated, "black women law professors need to keep past experiences in their minds as they speak in neither a whisper nor a shout."[47]

Joyce Hughes was certainly not the only African American woman law professor who has faced a hostile and isolating environment in the legal academy. Several of her contemporaries have recounted gripping and sometimes chilling accounts of marginalization, disrespect, and hostile behavior from colleagues. The intersection of race and gender remains a perennial factor in the lives of black women in the legal academy. Because of a less than receptive response from the legal academy, many black women law professors have sought out African American mentors, although sometimes this can end up being a frustrating experience. A number of the women interviewed state that they looked to people who had identical situations and endured similar struggles. As one black female law professor put it: "we look to people within our community to help, you know, in support of the kinds of things that we have to challenge, and many times I don't think there is much of a recognition that these are real and they have real consequences on us. And the fact that we can't rely on some of our colleagues for support is another element of the way that we feel put upon and challenged in these institutions."[48]

Taunya Lovell Banks is an African American woman law professor who entered the profession in 1976. Banks stated that her experience was rampant with tokenism. In an interview, she recalled the case of three African American women who were prominent in academic circles at the time. Two of them, Marilyn Yarborough and Mildred Robinson, looked very different from one another, Banks stated, yet they were frequently called by each other's name. The confusion over their identities went on over a long period of time. If there was a black person at a convention or meeting, it had to be this person or that person because black women law professors were so few in number and only a few of them were thought of having even minimal capacity to participate in such activities.[49]

Another problem that many black women in the legal academy have faced is that the *rules* are often changed in a manner that places many women, and particularly women of color, at a disadvantage. It is not as if these women are unable to adapt to the climate needed to succeed in the legal academy; however, unwritten rules are a part of many law schools, especially predominantly white law schools. Those who are part of the dominant white male culture are implicitly aware of these rules, but women, particularly women of color, are, at least initially, unaware of them. The result is that these women become increasingly marginalized in the academy and are put at a significant disadvantage when it comes time to be granted tenure, promotion, pay raises, department chairmanships, endowed chairs, and any other perks that are a part of the legal academy. For black women in the legal academy who are adept enough to acclimate to the rules for success, by the time they become aware of what these do's and don'ts are, it is often too late to reap the benefits. Often, the rules for success are explained to them in a convoluted manner.[50]

Another example of indifference and marginalization is that black women law professors are often isolated and are seen as invisible by their colleagues. Their experiences and stories are treated with indifference. Seldom is there any concern from nonblack colleagues about the physical or emotional well-being of black faculty. One black professor described a very stressful situation when she was recovering from a stroke. No one inquired about her health while she was on medical leave. No one asked her how she was doing when she returned to teaching.[51]

The perception of invisibility and marginalization was evident when this same professor asked for information related to faculty teaching loads. The professor was not asking for anything that was confidential. After waiting and receiving no reply, she called the associate dean. The associate dean informed her that the dean was determined not to divulge the information. Not satisfied with this response, she called the dean. It was two months before the dean finally replied that faculty could not be privy to the information and that faculty only received information similar to that of students. Because of this, the professor decided to distribute a memo to the entire faculty. This professor made no allegations or exhibited any anger. All she did was inform her colleagues that she was informed by the dean that no faculty would be able to get certain information about the number of credit hours they taught.[52]

She believed that if faculty were not allowed to know how many credit hours their peers taught, then her colleagues should be aware of this situation. Three of her colleagues responded to her. One invited her to his office and told her he did not know what was going on. He professed to being dumbfounded. The second was a senior faculty member who kept his own data. The third was a young, conservative, white male who professed to having no standing, but he was prepared to tell the dean that she should be allowed to have such information. Apparently this young, white, conservative law professor realized that he possessed more clout than she did as a black female senior law professor.[53]

Another professor, Annette Gordon-Reed, argued that it is imperative for black faculty to have earned their degrees from top institutions, otherwise they are ignored. She believed that this is one way of compensating for being black. She also argues that the standards are not quite as rigorous for whites as they are for blacks. Although she was a stellar performer at NYU School of Law, was a member of the law review, and was at the top of her class, she was unable to get a job in a New York City law firm. She attributes her exclusion to not being from the "correct or, better yet, required" schools for blacks—Harvard, Yale, Columbia, Stanford, for example. Virtually all blacks who desired to work at these firms had to come from these schools. Whites, on the other hand, could come from less prestigious institutions.[54] This happened despite the fact that she graduated from a first-rate law school. For black people, attending a solid law school is not good enough. You have to be from an ivy-league law school or ivy-league equivalent. A number of women have argued that black women in the legal academy are viewed with more scrutiny than black men, and in some cases are seen as more suspect.[55]

Another example of a hostile work environment is one described by Taunya Lovell Banks, who discussed an incident that took place when she was alone in a faculty lounge. A white male faculty member came in and told her, "Oh, I'm surprised you're at school today. I thought that you would be taking a holiday." "Why would you think that?" she responded. "Isn't this Lincoln's birthday?" he said. The callousness of such a remark was maliciously intended. Banks stated that those sorts of incidents frequently take place. "They wait until you get alone or are isolated to make hateful kinds of comments like that, to let you know, no matter what, you are not wanted."[56] Banks's story was similar to that of many of her contemporaries. Many of these women argued that their presence on their respective faculties reminded their more bigoted colleagues of their own prejudices and inadequacies. Joyce Hughes spoke of an incident where the clerical staff referred to her by her first name, yet referred to her colleagues as professor. This prompted her to notify the dean, requesting that he "please instruct the clerical staff that until they begin the practice of calling all other professors by their first name, they can refrain from calling me Joyce and address me as Professor Hughes."[57] Over time, such experiences take their toll, both psychologically and emotionally.[58]

These are just a few examples of the disrespectful behavior that causes black women in the legal academy to develop a sense that many of their colleagues do not have their best interests at heart and would actively work to undermine or damage their careers. It would be difficult to argue that Banks's colleague was acting out of benign ignorance when he made his obnoxious comment about Lincoln's birthday. He saw himself as a white male who had a position of power, no matter how minimal, over a black woman who was in an isolated position. Thus, he exercised his power to insult someone he felt was unworthy of respect.

Ironically, despite such disrespectful behavior, Banks argued that the majority of white law faculty at southern law schools prefer black faculty as opposed to having other faculty of color. Banks believed that despite deeply ingrained stereotypes, there is a certain degree of familiarity with blacks among southern whites that is not prevalent with other groups of color.[59] In other words, black people are the "devil we know." Latinos, Arabs, Pacific Islanders, Asians, and other minorities are too recent for southern whites to have developed a comfortable relationship with them. Religion undoubtedly is another factor as well. That the majority of southern blacks and whites are Christians presents a commonality that is absent from most other groups of color with the exception of Latinos.

Virtually all the law professors interviewed either heard or witnessed a white colleague make sexist or racist comments in their presence or in departmental meetings. Interestingly, many of these women stated that departmental meetings were where potentially volatile encounters took place. Most of the disrespectful behavior was sophisticated. Several of the professors believe that some white deans and others in high-level administration positions were reluctant to be seen as too supportive to black law faculty due to the fact that they would possibly be perceived by their white peers as "troublemakers" or "too committed to diversity."[60] A few of the professors argued that at some point, no matter how subtle, some colleague will make an effort to exercise white arrogance privilege. A white colleague in a meeting will quietly try to discredit a remark the black faculty member made, even if the comment was sound. A faculty member in a different area of expertise will attempt to prove that they are more of an expert on the subject matter than the black faculty member who has specialized in the field. The message of such boorish behavior is: "Although you may think you are powerful, you are not. I am more powerful than you and I can take away any authority you have anytime I want."[61]

Due to what they see as a hostile environment, some black professors decide to distance themselves from other black faculty as a survival mechanism. Many of them quickly realize that this usually results in a failed strategy.[62] One professor reached out to a fellow black female colleague on her law faculty, but the woman refused to make any effort to reciprocate. The only black male on the faculty invited her to lunch only once during a several-year period. The professor chalks this experience up to a number of factors and speculates that being in a less than supportive environment probably contributed to her colleagues' aloof attitudes.[63]

One law professor spoke of being so depressed and emotionally drained by hearing so many insensitive comments that she eventually "divorced" herself from her faculty. This decision did not happen overnight. She eventually went to her dean and told him that they were not paying her enough for her to have to hear the racist and sexist slurs she was hearing at committee meetings. She made it clear that such an environment was interfering with her scholarship and taking a toll on her emotionally. While a more ideal situation would have been for her colleagues to refrain from engaging in such insensitive behavior, she refused to take that chance. Rather than take a "wait and see" attitude, the professor decided that she was the one who had to initiate action. She made the decision to say that those people would no longer be a part of her community. These individuals were merely people who worked in her building.[64]

Many of these women argue that having to deal with such stressful situations and with petty, bigoted, hostile, disrespectful colleagues makes them feel more justified in earning the salaries that they do. Some, like Banks, believe that the cost of living in an integrated environment, going to school and living in an integrated, elitist community, is far greater than their grandparents or even their own parents could ever anticipate.[65] Interestingly, some of the first wave of black women legal scholars found that they were unprepared for the work conditions they were placed in. Some were fortunate in being children of segregation and then the civil rights movement. With the words of sagacious advice from forebears, they were armed with protective devices that they believe are absent from some of the younger black women (and men) who are entering the legal academy. Their self-confidence is stronger.[66]

Judy Scales-Trent, a biracial woman with very light skin, looks white. In her book *Notes of a White, Black Woman*, Scales-Trent, a professor of law at SUNY-Buffalo, recited two provocative incidents where she experienced disrespectful behavior from white colleagues.

> I was at a dessert party with some old-old friends and friends of theirs whom I am meeting for the first time. All White. While talking with one of the men, the topic turned to civil rights issues. Even more treacherous, the topic turned to affirmative action. In an attempt to warn him that racist comments would be inappropriate, in an attempt to avoid having to leave the party after such comments, I let him know that I was Black. But clearly he had been fore-warned, because he was not surprised. He was, indeed, ready. And he replied, with a smile: "No, you're not."[67]

The man's refusal to believe that she was indeed black is not all that surprising to Scales-Trent. She argued that many whites harbor the belief that any black person who resembles them in appearance, speaks the King's English, and is comfortable speaking with white people cannot possibly be black. Yet the experience at the party made an indelible impression on Scales-Trent. She was stunned by what she saw as "the sense of entitlement" that many white people harbor. The man at the party felt totally comfortable letting her know that it was he (a white man) who would tell her (a biracial woman) who she was. She was prohibited from identifying herself.[68]

An example of disrespectful and marginalizing behavior outside of the halls of the legal academy occurred when Scales-Trent was at the scene of a cab accident where the driver whose cab she was in crashed into two cars. As a police officer was taking down information from Scales-Trent, she informed him that he had made a mistake in checking her racial identity as white. He gave her a long, bored look, decided not to engage in a discussion with her, and told her, "If you say so." Scales-Trent recounts that she was livid at what she saw as his condescending behavior. It was as if it was some perverted idea of hers to refer to herself as black.[69]

The mistaken perception of black women as wanton women who are incapable of being mentored and unworthy of respect has been an issue for a number of black women in the legal academy. Black women face daunting challenges. A number of white men often express doubts about their ability to mentor a black female.[70] Black women also must deflect any suggestion that they are sleeping with senior white male colleagues, especially those who are in positions of authority. Many white women have to be concerned about this assumption as well. In fact, this charge is usually levied against white women more so than black women.[71]

A number of black women in the legal academy have been the victim of sexual harassment and disrespectful behavior from white male colleagues. Anita Allen, a distinguished professor at the University of Pennsylvania School of Law and prolific academic, experienced this during her early years as a law student. Allen excelled academically in her classes. The majority of her grades were excellent. Socially, the situation for her was more complex. The environment that she inhabited was a more traditional department of white male professors; moreover, some of these professors were not above sexual harassment and gender bias. Because she was female, and perhaps due to preconceived stereotypes they held about black women, some of the professors viewed Allen as fair game, as someone who would or should be receptive to their advances. It was difficult for Allen to establish herself as a serious intellectual in such an environment. One professor literally closed his door and chased Allen around his office with his lips puckered. Moreover, she had to fire her dissertation chairman because he grabbed her and attempted to kiss her during their first meeting. Some of the professors could not rise above the notion that Allen was a sex object.[72]

Anita Hill provided an account of her first year as a professor at the University of Oklahoma School of Law and the less than supportive environment she encountered. The common complaint was that she had been hired due to affirmative action. In the law school environment, any perceived error in her teaching or attitude toward the students was viewed as evidence of her supposed incompetence. Rumors about student reactions to her calling on them in the classroom included comments such as "You don't have to answer to a nigger," or "That nigger doesn't know anything." One administrator told Hill that he relied on "hall talk" from the students in evaluating her first year of teaching.[73]

A number of black female law professors described how the factor of isolation impacted them. Judy Scales-Trent recalled that during her first year, she frequently floundered and erred. Concerned about her performance and unbeknownst to her, a university administrator sought out a white colleague in the hope that her situation could be rectified. Scales-Trent later learned that the colleague in question told the administrator that he could not assist her due to the fact that he "did not know how to talk to her" since she was "not from the street." Instead of her difference being an asset, her "sameness" became a liability. She was not "authentic" enough.[74]

Not all of the professors interviewed saw their job as entirely filled with hostile encounters. Kimberly Jade Norwood states that in general, she has been pretty satisfied with her job and had a good experience at her institution. However, Norwood is quick to acknowledge that, as any racially astute black person in America can attest, there are moments when she is well aware that a white person would probably be treated more respectfully in a given situation. Norwood argued that stereotypes, prejudices, and biases are rampant throughout the culture. She states that this is a reality for black people in America, whether some blacks want to admit it or not.[75]

Beverly Moran believed that the legal academy presents both pleasant and hostile experiences simultaneously for black women.[76] One black female professor who has taught at two very prestigious law schools located in different parts of the nation says that while, in general, she was treated respectfully, in a few cases she encountered students who gave her less respect than they did her white male counterparts. In some cases, they were outright hostile toward her.

Some professors believe there is a double standard in the popular culture arena. Moreover, a level of irony seems to exist if such rhetoric is being espoused at a time when universities are having trouble dealing with issues of free speech, hate crimes, sexual harassment, racial harassment, and other vices. The climate of reaction by many universities and the general legal climate suggests that there would be very little that universities could do to maintain order, to maintain a kind of civil educational environment for all people. Thus, there is a large degree of hypocrisy.[77] Political correctness is an issue of concern to many of these law professors. The majority of them see it as a political controversy that has spun considerably out of control.[78] Others, like Lani Guinier, see it a red herring.[79] Some see it as a tool employed by the far right to silence a number of progressive scholars, not just in the legal academy, but in the academy in general, mainly women and women of color.[80]

Many of these women, such as Taunya Lovell Banks, Judy Scales-Trent, and Kimberlé Crenshaw, believe that progressive scholars are the primary targets of the political correctness movement and are victimized considerably by it. The downside of such a retrograde reaction, according to these professors, is that it curtails what seems to be a promising time of intellectual thought in both the legal academy and academia in general.[81] The legal academy seems to have gotten to the point where it is beginning to have just the inklings of a critical mass, enough people involved in various areas of scholarship to be able to develop some very new, interesting, emerging disciplines, aspects of scholarship, new kinds of thoughts, things that would not have been possible a decade earlier. Ironically, just as all this new scholarship, new thinking, new energy starts to emerge, particularly from people of color and from women and women of color, the political correctness movement seems to effectively deride and target progressive scholars and have a negative impact on such scholarship. Many of these academics feel isolated due to such reactions.[82]

While many of these women decry the antiprogressive politics of the political correctness movement, they are very pleased with the emphasis that has been placed on multiculturalism. Several of these women argued that people constantly need to be exposed to those who are different, and that the study and inclusion of individuals of various cultures, races, and ethnicities is a positive factor for the academy. Kimberly Jade Norwood believed that we live in a diverse and pluralistic society, and that our law schools should reflect this fact. Norwood further argued that if people are forced to see other ways of thinking, points of view, cultures, and experiences, such encounters ultimately contribute to their thinking, and that such mass exposure to different cultures can help ameliorate negative stereotypes.[83] The fact that many individuals in the multicultural movement place a significant emphasis on women is important as well.[84]

There is no doubt that multiculturalism has had many beneficial effects. It has had many focuses of attention, sometimes in curricular development as well as coverage in academic disciplines. Some professors are supportive of multiculturalism and other forms of diversity but caution that such movements can be used as a double-edged sword. Beverly Moran says that ideas such as multiculturalism have made it possible for many people of color to have jobs they would otherwise not have access to. However, she argued that it has created feelings of ambiguity in people of color who do not want to be associated with race and feel that any reference to race impacts upon them in a negative manner. Moran believes that the downside of such programs is that they can be used in a negative way to advance agendas that are less than noble.[85] There is no doubt that certain entities can be a divisive tool in the hands of the wrong people.

Given the historical legacy of groups in the United States that have been marginalized and deprived of rights, it is important to acknowledge that only through due process was such a movement able to come to fruition in the legal academy. Dorothy Roberts argued that more often than not, individuals and groups who discuss issues of victimization and marginalization are often justified in their concerns and usually do not employ exploitive tactics to promote their agenda. She believed that people of color and gays and lesbians are victims of systematic oppression and discrimination and must aggressively work to end such victimization.[86]

Even before the days of multiculturalism and political correctness, there were always some white professors who were committed to increasing the level of diversity in the legal academy. Many of the law professors interviewed mentioned that some liberal law professors made strategic moves to better institutions (many of them to ivy-league institutions) so that when these younger faculty women went up for tenure, they could receive letters from Harvard, Yale, Stanford, the University of Chicago, and other premier law schools. Many of these women were committed to academic careers from the onset. While they acknowledge that there were racist and sexist professors who resented the presence of people of color and women in the legal academy, they were able to overcome such obstacles. A number of these women argue that they lived in a state of grace in regard to liberal whites after they became full-fledged academics, but also became astute to the limitations of white liberalism, yet were largely immune to such politics while they were students.[87]

Professional jealousy is another problem that some of these women encountered. This was certainly true in the case of those who were prolific in their scholarship, were well regarded by their students, and were thought of positively by administrators and the larger community.[87] Some of these women heard remarks that their scholarship was adequate but not great, or that they published in lower-level law journals. A number of these women also acknowledge that they have had some positive experiences with white colleagues and in the legal academy. Some express satisfaction in having the opportunity to collaborate with such colleagues on exciting academic projects and committee assignments, a certain degree of freedom that the legal academy affords them, and the flexibility that such an environment gives many of the senior tenured law faculty.

While these positive attributes of the legal academy are acknowledged, many of these professors still make clear that a feeling of superiority exists among many of their white colleagues. The "how dare you consider yourself equal to me," "how dare you challenge me" mindset is still prevalent, especially among white men.[88] As many struggle to combat isolation and marginalization, and to obtain a level of respect, the intersection of race and gender is an ever dominant force.

Notes

1. Interview with Joyce Hughes, June 26, 1997.
2. J. Clay Smith Jr., *Emancipation: The Making of the Black Lawyer, 1844–1944* (Philadelphia: University of Pennsylvania Press 1993). Lytle is the first woman of any race to teach at a chartered law school in the nation's history. In 1886, a year before she became a law professor, Ellen Spencer Mussey, white, and Emma Gillett, also white but a graduate of Howard University's law school, instructed students in their

law office. See also Herma Hill Kay, "The Future of Women Law Professors," *Iowa Law Review* 77 (1991): 5–6. According to Kay, the first woman tenure-track law professor at an ABA-approved and AALS school was Barbara Nachtrieb Armstrong, who was appointed an instructor in law and social economics at the University of California, Berkeley, in 1922.

3. Kay, "The Future of Women Law Professors," 9.

4. Emma Coleman-Jordan, "Images of Black Women in the Legal Academy: An Introduction," *Berkeley Women's Law Journal* 6 (1990–1991): 1, 13.

5. Hughes interview.

6. Frances Beale, "Double Jeopardy: To Be Black and Female," in *The Black Woman*, ed. Toni Cade (New York, American Library, 1970), 90–100.

7. American Bar Association, *A Review of Legal Education in the United States* (ABA Section of Legal Education and Admissions to the Bar, 1994), 67.

8. *Journal of Blacks in Higher Education* (Winter 1994–1995): 29. For a collection of essays by black women law professors, see "Symposium: Images of Black Women in the Legal Academy," *Berkeley Women's Law Journal* (1990–1991).

9. Brian Anderson, "Three Women Named by 'U' Regents," *Minneapolis Tribune*, April 17, 1971, 1A; Floyd Egner, "Regents Appoint 3 Women during 'Nonroutine' Session," *Minneapolis Daily*, April 19, 1971; "First Black Woman Graduate of 'U' Law School Named," *Minneapolis Spokesman*, April 22, 1971, 1; "Joyce Hughes to Join Law School Faculty," *Twin Cities Courier*, April 24, 1971, 1; "Black Woman to Join Law School Faculty," *University of Minnesota Alumni News*, May, 1971, 50. See also "At the University of Minnesota Law School: A 'Together' Prof.," *Ebony*, May 1972, 39.

10. Editorial, *Minneapolis Star*, April 19, 1971.

11. *Black Times* (Albany, Calif.), August 1971, 18. Hughes's response was quoted as "it is important that the brothers know that I do not want to gain one inch at their expense. We cannot allow a wedge to be driven between us for mutual respect and shared responsibility is essential in the struggle for liberation." See also Barbara J. Williams, "Black Women in Law," *Black Law Journal* 1 (1971): 171, in which the author emphatically states, "There is no problem between black men and black women. The problem is between black people and white society."

12. ABA, *A Review of Legal Education*, 67. Total J.D. enrollment was 91,225, of which women were 8,567. Of that number, 4,326 were first-year students.

13. Edward L. Littlejohn and Leonard S. Rubinowitz, "Black Enrollment in Law Schools: Forward to the Past," *Thurgood Marshall Law Review* 12 (1987): 415, 435. Total enrollment was 91,225, with black enrollment being 3,744, or 4.1 percent. However, these were all ABA-approved law schools, which would include some predominantly black law schools.

14. Stacey M. Brooks and Maurice Foster, "Another Dimension," *NBA Magazine*, September 1992, 20.

15. Speaking of being both black and female in their early years in the profession, Patricia King of Georgetown said, "The combination is deadly, or can be deadly. I

catch it from both sides. . . . I have found that being a woman as well as black is a double barrier." Proceedings of Minority Group Law Teachers Planning Conference, September 19–20, 1974, Harvard Law School, *Black Law Journal* 4 (1974): 575, 584. See generally, "Symposium: Black Women Law Professors: Building a Community at the Intersection of Race and Gender," *Berkeley Women's Law Journal* (1991). For all "people of color" law professors, Reginald L. Robinson said, "we get questioned more, doubted often and dismissed quickly." *AALS Section on Minority Groups Newsletter*, October 1995, 2.

16. AALS, Proceedings 1973, Report of Section on Minority Groups. More than ten years after this event, the added duties of minority faculty still existed. See Derrick Bell and Richard Delgado, "Minority Law Professor's Lives: The Bell-Delgado Survey," *Harvard Civil Rights and Civil Liberties Law Review* 24:2 (1989): 349, 352. See also Cheryl I. Harris, "Law Professors of Color and the Academy: Of Poets and Kings," *Chicago-Kent Law Review* 68 (1992): 331, 342.

17. Hughes interview.

18. "Request to the Dean," *Minneapolis Daily*, November 18, 1974, 8 (letter to editor, signed by ninety-two law students). See also Carl A. Auerbach, "Dean Clarifies Stand, *Minneapolis Daily*, November 18, 1974, 9 (letter to editor); "Auerbach Reiterates Questioned Lecture," *Minneapolis Daily*, November 19, 1974, 1; "Auerbach's Sincerity Questioned about AA," *Twin City Observer*, November 20, 1974, 1; Carl A. Auerbach, "The Silent Opposition of Professors and Graduate Students to Preferential Affirmative Action Programs: 1969 and 1975," *Minnesota Law Review* 72 (1988): 1233.

19. Hughes interview.

20. The University of Minnesota Law School Faculty Minutes, September 29, 1972, record that "Professors Hughes and Schoettle were neutral on the issue and that the Scholastic Requirements committee had voted 3 to 2 to recommend approval. A motion was made to permit the students in Legal Professions to opt for a pass-fail grading system. The motion was seconded and following discussion failed of passage, thus leaving the course on the normal grading system."

21. According to Hughes, "the other section was taught by a white male. There were 134 students in my section. Ninety persons signed the petition, but in response to a question at the hearing, the dean acknowledged that no one had checked the signatures on the petition to determine if they were in fact students in my class." Hughes has a copy of the draft minutes of the University of Minnesota Law School Faculty Meeting of June 11, 1973. No final minutes of that meeting were ever made or adopted, but the entire proceeding was tape-recorded.

22. Hughes interview.

23. Hughes took issue with the notion that the course was "subjective." She finds the term a pejorative way of saying that something taught by a black woman imparts a perspective different from that of a white male. Even the white male teaching the other section testified on her behalf before the Grievance Committee about the nature of the course. Hughes interview.

24. Hughes interview. Letter from Loftus E. Becker Jr. to Joyce A. Hughes, April 13, 1974.

25. Her first year teaching the course, the other professor had proposed that he and Hughes both go to a Pass/Fail system, but Hughes did not agree. She did not know what involvement, if any, he had in the initial student petition to the faculty, which was directed at both their sections. At the faculty meeting that acted on the petition, he was "neutral."

26. Hughes interview.

27. Memorandum from Joyce A. Hughes to the Faculty, December 14, 1972.

28. Memorandum from BALSA to the Faculty, January 19, 1973.

29. Hughes interview.

30. Hughes interview.

31. "Minority teachers can expect difficulties from many white students who have never had a non-white peer, much less a non-white in a position of authority over them." Proceedings of Minority Group Law Teachers Planning Conference, 577. See also Derrick Bell, *Confronting Authority—Reflections of an Ardent Protester* (Boston: Beacon, 1994).

32. While the Grievance Committee denied the requested Pass/Fail grading, it nonetheless entertained the issue of competency and made gratuitous remarks that BALSA said "leaves a very negative impression of Professor Hughes' performance and ability as a teacher." BALSA memo to the faculty. The memo also states: "We further object strenuously to the negative innuendoes and free extemporizing in the final section of the report. It is transparent that this is a subtle attempt to find fault where none had been shown."

33. In his article on affirmative action, Auerbach says: "Silence is interpreted as agreement." Auerbach, "The Silent Opposition," 1278. Hughes rejoins: "Certainly I did not want him or the faculty to assume acquiescence based upon silence by me." She also quotes Derrick Bell's comment that "silent suffering does not beget reform." Bell, "Introduction to Delgado," 350.

34. The Grievance Committee did question whether the requested action was an appropriate remedy, assuming incompetence could be shown. Despite doubts about the requested remedy, the committee then proceeded to determine matters of competency.

35. Hughes interview.

36. Letter from Carl A. Auerbach to Joyce A. Hughes, March 4, 1974.

37. Hughes interview.

38. According to Hughes, Northwestern's law library had black staff, many secretaries were black, and at the time, all the maintenance people at the law school were black. In contrast, there were no African Americans working in any capacity at the University of Minnesota Law School other than Hughes.

39. Hughes interview. The Minnesota dean expressed a hope "that the year at Northwestern will help you to gain perspective on your problems." Letter from Carl A. Auerbach to Joyce A. Hughes, October 1, 1974. Hughes responded to Auerbach

that it was "disappointing for you to suggest that this year will only be of benefit to me in my problems," noting that "those problems are shared by the University of Minnesota, if not caused by it." Letter from Joyce A. Hughes to Carl A. Auerbach, October 16, 1974.

40. Hughes interview. Several other law professors interviewed echoed similar comments.

41. At the time of this interview, Hughes stated that at least six blacks (five women and one man) were now law professors who had been students at North-western Law School during the time she taught there. While she did nothing directly to cause them to choose law teaching, she believes her presence helped them to see law teaching as a viable career option, if only subconsciously.

42. Hughes's career benefited from people who took actions not then usual. There was Jane Andrews, placement director at Carleton College, Northfield, Minnesota; Judge Earl R. Larson, U.S. District Court, District of Minnesota; Herbert Lefler of the firm of Lefler, Lefevere, et al.; Dean William B. Lockhart, University of Minnesota Law School 1956–1972; Dean James A. Rahl, Northwestern University School of Law 1972–1977; and former Supreme Court Justice (1962–65) Arthur Goldberg, head of the U.S. delegation to the 1977 Belgrade, Yugoslavia, conference on the Helsinki Accord.

43. Hughes interview.

44. Hughes interview. See also Kimberlé Williams Crenshaw, "Foreword: Toward a Race-Conscious Pedagogy in Legal Education," *Black Law Journal* 11 (1989), reprinted in *Southern California Review of Law and Women's Studies* 4 (1994): 33, 35.

45. Hughes interview. According to Hughes, a white male student related that he and others felt more comfortable in her classes than others taught by white male professors and thus participated more. She is also aware, however, that some students may feel they have license to "question more, doubt often and dismiss quickly" in a class taught by a black woman.

46. Hughes interview.

47. Joyce Hughes "Neither a Whisper nor a Shout," in *Rebels in Law: Voices in the History of Black Women Lawyers*, ed. J. Clay Smith Jr. (Ann Arbor: University of Michigan Press, 1988), 93–95.

48. Interview with Kimberlé Crenshaw, March 12, 1999.

49. Interview with Taunya Lovell Banks, March 18, 1998.

50. Several of the law professors interviewed stated these experiences as the norm about the environment of the legal academy.

51. Hughes interview.

52. Hughes interview.

53. Hughes interview.

54. Interview with Annette Gordon-Reed, January 5, 2001.

55. Hughes "Neither a Whisper nor a Shout," 92.

56. Banks interview.

57. Hughes interview.

58. A number of the law professors interviewed described stories of other black women who have suffered from depression, anger, and other problems related to a stressful environment.

59. Banks interview.

60. Hughes, "Neither a Whisper nor a Shout," 92.

61. Banks interview.

62. Interview with Judy Scales-Trent, February 19, 1997.

63. Scales-Trent interview.

64. Scales-Trent interview.

65. Banks interview.

66. Interview with Anita Allen, February 24, 1997; Banks interview.

67. Judy Scales-Trent, *Notes of a White, Black Woman: Race, Color, Community* (University Park: Pennsylvania State University Press, 1995), 73.

68. Scales-Trent, *Notes of a White, Black Woman*, 73.

69. Scales-Trent, *Notes of a White, Black Woman*, 74.

70. Several of the law professors interviewed, Anita Allen, Taunya Lovell Banks, Annette Gordon-Reed, Paulette Caldwell, and Joyce Hughes, echoed this belief.

71. Hughes "Neither a Whisper nor a Shout," 92.

72. Allen interview.

73. Anita Hill, *Speaking Truth to Power* (Doubleday: New York, 1997), 88.

74. Scales-Trent, *Notes of a White, Black Woman*, 123.

75. Interview with Kimberly Jade Norwood, August 19, 2007.

76. Interview with Beverly Moran, September 3, 2007.

77. Moran interview.

78. Anita Allen, Lani Guinier, Annette Gordon-Reed, and Kimberlé Crenshaw in particular believe that political correctness has been a tool employed by the political right to discredit progressive thought in academia.

79. Interview with Lani Guinier, May 15, 1997.

80. Taunya Lovell Banks, Judy Scales-Trent, Anita Allen, and several other black law professors echoed this sentiment.

81. Banks interview; Trent interview; Crenshaw interview.

82. Banks interview.

83. Norwood interview.

84. All of the women lawyers interviewed stated this belief.

85. Moran interview.

86. Interview with Dorothy Roberts, September 20, 2007.

87. Allen interview; Banks interview; Gordon-Reed interview.

88. Banks interview; Crenshaw interview; Hughes interview.

89. Allen interview; Banks interview; Crenshaw interview; Hughes interview; Scales-Trent interview.

CHAPTER THREE

~

Dealing with the Multiple Isms: Racism, Sexism, Elitism

Being marginalized, devalued, and isolated can be a demoralizing experience for many black women in the legal academy, especially if compounded with racism, sexism, and other isms. Many radical activists argue that racism, like cancer or diabetes, is a disease. To people of color and women, who are often the victims of racism, white supremacy, and gender oppression, race and gender are major factors through which they view the larger world. The majority of whites do not look at the world from this perspective of being racially aware, despite the fact that they are representative of a race. The majority of whites, especially white men, have the luxury of ignoring how issues of race and gender impact upon their lives. But their race and gender afford them a societal advantage, sparing them from the damaging psychological effects that racism and sexism can cause, distinct from any advantage received from the existence of discriminatory racism.[1]

Cultural critic and black feminist bell hooks described her realization of the connection between these two concepts: "The word racism ceased to be the term which best expressed for me exploitation of black people and other people of color in this society and . . . I began to understand that the most useful term was white supremacy." Hooks also observed that many whites who believe that they are progressive on racial issues are often in denial on the extent to which they themselves foster racial prejudice through their own behavior, which is often condescending, paternalistic, and arrogant. She argued that many white liberals fail to see how they contribute to and benefit from a society that is rooted in white supremacy.[2] Legal scholars Stephanie

Wildman and Trina Grillo argued that "white supremacy" is an important term, descriptive of American social reality.[3] During my interviews with each of these law professors, two factors would always be prevalent in the experiences of these women—the issues of racism and sexism. In every interview, it was clear that the perpetuation of racism, sexism, or white supremacy was evident in the experiences of these women.[4]

These women law professors gave countless examples that whatever the setting—the legal academy, conferences, public forums—whenever a colleague, guest speaker, or student discussed sexism and racism, the significance of race was marginalized or obscured, and the impact of the role that race played in the lives of people of color and whites was overlooked. More than often, the grievances of their white counterparts, as opposed to their own concerns, took precedence as the basis for discussion. A number of black women academics have discussed how this mindset is a perennial phenomenon in various settings. Furthermore, any discussion of gender issues was assumed to be related to white women, while racial topics were associated as the province of black men. Finally, people with little experience in thinking about racism or white supremacy, but who had a hard-won understanding of an allegedly analogous oppression (sexism or some other ism), assumed that they comprehended the experience of people of color and thus had standing to speak on their behalf.[5] It was assumed that all women of color had the same experience.

Essentialism is implicit in analogies between sex and race. Legal scholar Angela Harris explains gender essentialism as the "notion that there is a monolithic 'women's experience' that can be described independent of other facets of experience like race, class, and sexual orientation." She continues, "A corollary to gender essentialism is 'racial essentialism'—the belief that there is a monolithic 'Black Experience,' or 'Chicano Experience.' "[6]

Black feminists Gloria Hall and Barbara Smith argued:

> To analogize gender to race, one must assume that each is a distinct category, the impact of which can be nearly separated, one from the other. The essentialist critique shows that this division is not possible. Whenever it is attempted, the experience of women of color, who are at the intersection of these categories and cannot divide themselves to compare their own experiences, is rendered invisible. Analogizing sex discrimination to race discrimination makes it seem that all the women are white and all the men are African American.[7]

"Moreover, feminist essentialism represents not just an insult to black women, but a broken promise—the promise to listen to women's stories, the promise of feminist method."[8]

No matter how carefully a setting was structured to address the question of racism or white supremacy, these problems always arose. Several of the women interviewed conceded that they were complicit in creating these problems on many occasions, yet when they tried to avoid them, they found themselves accused of making others uncomfortable. In short, the problem lay within them.[9]

A few began to question why this situation continued. A few came to the conclusion that these phenomena have much to do with the dangers inherent in what had previously seemed to them a creative and solidarity-producing process—analogizing sex discrimination to race discrimination. These dangers were marginalized by the belief that discussing and comparing oppressions may lead to coalition building and understanding. On an individual, psychological level, they sympathized and understood others by comparing the situations of others with some aspects of their own.

The majority of black women law professors interviewed believe that a number of their colleagues are decent, well-intentioned individuals, and that the majority are people with antiracist politics who have no desire to perpetuate racism or white supremacy. But even well-intentioned people may act unwittingly to maintain racism and white supremacy.

Legal scholars Stephanie Wildman and Trina Grillo argue:

> Comparing sexism to racism perpetuates patterns of racial domination by minimizing the impact of racism, rendering it as insignificant phenomenon, one of a laundry list of isms or oppressions that society must suffer. This marginalization and obfuscation is evident in three recognizable patterns: (1) the taking back of center stage from people of color, even in discussions of racism, so that white issues remain or become central in the dialogue; (2) the fostering of essentialism, so that women and people of color are implicitly viewed as belonging to mutually exclusive categories, rendering women of color invisible; and (3) the appropriation of pain or the denial of its existence that results when whites who have compared other oppressions to race discrimination believe they understand the experience of racism.[10]

A large number of whites (liberals as well as conservatives) believe that people of color are rabidly consumed with the issue of racial identity and in many cases are perplexed to see the inordinate amount of attention that some people of color devote in addressing the issue.[11] They do this while at the same time ignoring the fact that white domination and white supremacy afford them the opportunity to exploit, disregard, and frequently abnegate the issue of racism (in the case of white men, sexism as well) whenever they desire to do so.[12] Many whites need to relinquish their denial about racism and sexism and genuinely acknowledge that they do indeed benefit from the internal hierarchies in American society that afford white, particularly white male, privilege. Moreover, well-intentioned whites should not assume that assumed progressive attitudes about race make them qualified to speak on behalf of other minorities. Such a mind-set is arrogant and condescending.[13]

A number of professors interviewed argue that whites need to reject this privilege and recognize and speak about their role in the racial hierarchy.[14]

A number of academics who study race and gender issues have argued that white supremacy affords whites the assumption that the issues that are of paramount concern to them will be at the forefront in every discussion.[15] Frequently, problems occur when those who are in the dominant group (white) feel that others are attempting to usurp or marginalize their power or are treating them in a manner they deem disrespectful. The white, male, heterosexual societal norm is privileged in such a way that its privilege is rendered invisible. As Kimberlé Crenshaw explained, "According to a dominant view, a discriminator treats all people within a race or sex category similarly. Any significant experiential or statistical variation within this group suggests . . . that the group is not being discriminated against." Angela Harris states: "Race and sex . . . become significant only when they operate to explicitly *disadvantage* the victims; because the *privileging* of whiteness or maleness is implicit, it is generally not perceived at all."[16]

Because whiteness is the norm, it is easy to forget that it is not the only perspective. Thus, members of dominant groups assume that their perceptions are the valid ones, that their issues are the ones that need to be addressed, and that in any form of discussion, they should be the one speaking rather than listening to others speak. The advantage of being a member of a preferred group is being the center and the subject of all inquiry in which people of color or other marginalized groups are the objects.[17]

A couple of legal scholars have made the argument:

> So strong is this expectation of holding center stage that even when a time and place are specifically designated for members of a nonprivileged group to be central, members of the dominant group will often attempt to take back the pivotal focus. They are stealing the center—usually with a complete lack of self-consciousness.[18]

Indeed, one of the dangers in focusing on diversity is that it can direct attention only to a certain group or groups, for example, Asian Americans. People who have Asian backgrounds can be very different from each other. A Vietnamese refugee is in a very different category from a wealthy person of Japanese ancestry descended from several generations of Americans. Moreover, diversity can vary based on geographic region. At many West Coast colleges and universities, ethnic diversity can often mean Asian American students to the exclusion of African American and Latino students.[19]

It is obvious that racism, sexism, and the multiple isms were not overnight developments in the legal academy. These vices have been a major part of American society since its inception. As Judy Scales-Trent observed: "In 1780, this country enacted its first immigration and naturalization statute in which it said you can only become a naturalized citizen if you are white. I think this country has always been clear about who is supposed to be a citizen and who is not, and I don't think that has changed."[20]

It was interesting to note that a couple of the law professors interviewed admitted that they were unaware of being the victims of gender discrimination while they were graduate students. If such discrimination occurred, they were oblivious to it.[21] Others argued that even if they were unaware of being the victims of such treatment, they undoubtedly suffered from sexism due to the fact that they are women of color and it is impossible for them to separate their gender from their race.[22] They face the dual reality of "Jane and Jim Crow" that black female legal activist Pauli Murray mentions—black women and other women of color suffer racial and gender discrimination.[23] Kimberlé Crenshaw argues that Murray's definition is "the most profound way" of trying to express the experiences that women of color encounter.[24]

Figuratively speaking, trying to capture and challenge Jim Crow is widely regarded as a project that the majority of African Americans are engaged in, as was evident in the Anita Hill–Clarence Thomas hearings. Yet challenging Jane Crow is not an exercise that the overwhelming majority of African Americans are committed to or even believe that the larger community as a whole should be engaged in. It is the institutional fact that it exists and African Americans (particularly black women) have to deal with it, but also the fact that black women have to deal with often being marginalized in their own communities. Often, many African Americans look to people within their communities in an effort to help address the issues we need to challenge. For the most part, many black men (and more than a few women) do not view the issue of sexism—"Jane Crow"—to be an issue worthy of recognition, or realize how significant the problem is, and many fail to see the detrimental impact that such a vice can have on the community. Within the African American community there are people who are in positions to combat Jane Crow, yet they refuse to do so. Thus, many black women who are struggling against racism and sexism, both in the legal academy and at large, feel put upon.[25]

This attitude of indifference, or at the very least, ambivalence, toward the dilemmas that professional black women encounter was evident in the years following the Hill-Thomas hearings. There were not many black people falling out of the woodwork when Jocelyn Elders was dismissed as surgeon general by President Clinton. There was not an abundance of African Americans announcing their disgust in regard to the treatment of Lani Guinier. As many on the conservative right (and some on the political left) were referring to her as a "quota queen," there were not large numbers of black people standing up to defend Guinier and denouncing her treatment as racist. For many Americans, especially black Americans, gender politics is a distorting prism through which we see politics. When that is coupled with the tendency to think that color constitutes consciousness, you get a toxic form of race-conscious politics. Several of the law professors interviewed stated that they hope Clarence Thomas serves as a permanent example about the black community's need to redefine the boundaries of political solidarity, and for the community to be more sagacious in whom it lends its support to.[26] A number of the law professors believed that all aspects of the academy, including the legal academy, will always be a battleground where race, gender, and other related issues will be at the forefront of debate.

It was true throughout the 1980s and 1990s that discussions about the place of women and people of color in higher education, coupled with issues of quality and merit, became the yardstick for measuring the "value" of such groups. Such issues are going to always generate a good deal of controversy. From a historical standpoint, people of color, and many women for that matter, did not begin to enter mainstream higher education institutions until the mid-1970s. Prior to this time, the numbers were virtually abysmal and there was no valid basis on which to make any meaningful comparison. The controversy was about such groups having the opportunity to attend institutions that they had previously been denied admission to.[27]

The few blacks, Latinos, and women who began to enter previously white-male-dominated institutions of higher learning were learning how to acclimate in an environment that was more than often cold and hostile. In addition, many people of minority groups harbored a certain degree of suspicion toward one another. Due to these factors, these groups primarily segregated themselves and stayed quiet for a while. Once these groups became more securely nestled in the ivy halls of academia, they began to demand certain changes—greater financial aid assistance for lower-income families, ethnic studies programs, greater numbers of faculty of color, and other concessions. This sort of activism did not come quickly to the legal academy, but over time it did.

Lani Guinier was among the first wave of women to enter the legal academy. In her co-authored book *Becoming Gentlemen*, she discussed the sexism that she and other female law students endured at the hands of an older white male law professor. "He would come into the classroom at ten minutes after the hour and he would say 'good morning, gentlemen.' The first day of class he acknowledged that there were female students in the class and stated 'but you have to bear with me because I am a creature of habit and I've been teaching for many years and so I don't mean any offense, but as far as I'm concerned, you are all gentlemen.'" At the time, Guinier viewed his behavior as eccentric. Guinier also discussed other experiences she had with men once she was in the legal world. Some men (not all) clearly believed that women should not be in the legal world, and that there is a patriarchal model of traits a lawyer should embody.[28]

Part of this mindset, according to Guinier, is that what many people who are not white males may call male-dominated sexism is, in reality, the mass education of large numbers of people that promotes efficiency over a pedagogy. She argues that for many women and people of color, and for some men who are quiet, "traditional" methods of learning such as large lecture halls of 150–200 students are not always the best approach to learning. Yet what may seem sexist to nonwhite males and women is seen by the majority of white males as the "best and proper way of doing things."[29] In essence, old habits die hard.

Judy Scales-Trent stated that as an undergraduate student she did not experience racism or sexism. The institution she attended made a sincere effort to be friendly to black students, but there were only ten black students out of several hundred. Scales-Trent argued that she became much more aware of racism and sexism when she enrolled in law school in 1970. She could not conclude if they were more racist or more sexist.[30]

Scales-Trent has written about her experiences as an African American woman, of "being black and looking white," and thereby inhabiting both sides of the privilege dichotomy. As one who was used to being on the unprivileged side of the race dichotomy in some aspects of her life, she discussed how the privilege of being able-bodied allowed her to ignore the pain of an unprivileged woman in a wheelchair, humiliated in seeking access to a meeting place.[31] She realized that her role as the privileged one in that pairing likened her to whites in the racial pairing. The analogy helped her see the role of privilege and how it affects us, presenting another example of how comparisons are useful for promoting understanding. But this insight did not lead her to assume that she could speak for those who are physically challenged; rather, she realized that she needed to listen more carefully.

Scales-Trent believes that the current law school environment is slightly more favorable to white women. Their numbers are increasing steadily, and that will probably be the case for the foreseeable future. Scales-Trent speaks of the retrograde policies of her institution, where it was decades before they named a woman as associate dean of the law school, to head a committee, or even to teach a first-year course unless she was married to a man who was popular. However, she conceded that her institution has done a very good job in addressing gender discrimination. This, she argues, is evident in the fact more than half the students at her institution are women.[32]

Anita Allen argued that black women are often treated as if they are more impervious than their white female counterparts. Anita Allen and Kimberly Jade Norwood both believe that there has been a more concerted effort in the legal academy to recognize diverse styles of teaching, classroom performance, and measurement of performance.[33] For women law faculty, such issues become gendered. These are the sort of second- and third-generation problems of feminism and sexism that the legal academy is now confronted with.[34] The majority of women interviewed share the belief that if a black faculty member's credentials are perceived as strong, they are perceived to be engaged in "legitimate" scholarship, or if the majority of white law faculty members are convinced that they hired the "right" black faculty member, then relationships among the groups tend to be tranquil. Issues are not brought up.[35]

It is important to note that Anita Allen credits Title VII of the 1964 Civil Rights Act for having a considerable impact on higher education. Moreover, she dismisses critics who argue that *Brown v. Board*[36] and related cases had very little impact on social change. She credited the very existence of the law itself, the considerable legislation under it, and the level of pressure that women and people of color exerted. The feeling that they could finally exert some pressure because of the existence of the law has had a lot to do with change. Allen believed that there is an educative impact to law, even when there has been less than one would desire in terms of actual compensation or actual numbers of trials or findings of discrimination against particular companies.

Allen mentioned the Texaco case of 1997 as a case in point in litigation. Embarrassed by the assumption that they were a company rife with racism and sexism, Texaco hurried up and made a settlement to get its name off the front pages of major newspapers and off the nightly news programs. There was no doubt that it was a public relations disaster. Millions of Americans of all races were prepared to boycott Texaco. They did not like the sense that there appeared to be a subversion of the law, a deliberate disregard for the law by high-placed executives, a kind of game playing with things that people hold dear. People have a real connection to legislation and to court decisions like *Brown*. Whether they should have one or not, they do. They have a connection to Title VII of the Civil Rights Act and a connection to the ideas that are behind particular cases, especially pieces of legislation. Allen argued that Title VII benefited minority men as well.[37]

Reflecting on her own segregated history, Allen spoke of being the product of a Jim Crow kindergarten, which was a lonely experience for her. When her family moved to Atlanta, Georgia, in the mid-1960s, she attended an integrated public high school where she was frequently called "nigger." During this time, there was also the issue of whether she would be able to attend one of the white public high schools near her home. She had to deal with exclusion from social activities, not being able to go to a skating rink because it was not the day "set aside for blacks." She dealt with a lot of segregation and half-hearted integration. However, Allen believed that a combination of her military background and the good fortune of being born after *Brown* made her life easier than the lives of her predecessors who came of age in the 1940s and 1950s.[38] Judy Scales-Trent mentioned that she entered Northwestern University in 1970, when they had just decided to bring in a larger number of black students, and this was fifteen years after *Brown*. She argued that, had it not been for *Brown*, they would not have made such a move.[39]

Patricia Williams recalled her days as an undergraduate:

Being Black at Wellesley had not prepared me for this aspect of life in the law. But then being Black at Wellesley might have been a completely anomalous experience at any moment before or since. I matriculated during a time when many Whites were still romanticizing the project of inclusion. There were so few of us Blacks that White classmates would come up and apologize to us for all the pain they imagined we were suffering. They wanted to know what it was *like* being Black. People wanted to invite you home for the specific purpose of shocking their parents. They would shyly offer to date your brother to show their solidarity with Black causes. And Lord knows *their* brothers missed no opportunity to play the Rolling Stones hit "Brown Sugar" over and over and then some again. (The personal was political was kind of a new notion back then.)[40]

Anita Hill says that she decided to attend Yale Law School over Harvard after visiting both campuses. Her decision was based on the fact that Yale was the smaller of the two law schools and provided her with a feeling of protection and security that she would need as a small-town woman who was making the transformation from a public to private institution. However, once she arrived on the Yale campus, she became aware that the smaller size of the institution only compensated so much for the relentless feeling of being an outsider.

However much those who direct the educational process perceive it as race and gender neutral, Yale cannot escape its history. (In many respects, it does not want to.) It was designed for young White men of privilege and only began to admit women in 1969. From its secret societies to its Whiffenpoofs, men dominated the culture of the institution in the 1970s, just as they had historically. And if we never spoke of class, status, or distinctions in the background, it was because they were so clearly taken for granted."[41]

Relationships with their white female cohorts was an issue of interest for many of these women. While the majority of these women found them to be positive on the whole, there were those who saw such relations as tepid at best. Anita Allen felt that while relationships between black and white women in the legal academy were good, that there was a tendency for white women to pigeonhole black women, or to call on black women only when they thought it was important to have a "black view." Many white women make an effort to respect black women for their individuality and differences; however, this often means that sometimes they make assumptions based on long-held stereotypes that are not always true. Allen argued that white women need to be more conscious in terms of egalitarian sharing.[42] Dorothy Roberts believed that black women have usually been able to find like-minded white women with whom they could align themselves. Roberts felt that there have been many examples of collaborations between women of both races on various projects that are of interest to women in general.[43]

Many black women law professors experienced racism in the way that courses were designed or the way that they were treated as students. Prior to the 1990s, there was very little effort to address sexism and racism in the legal academy. Many of these women credit the attention given to multiculturalism and diversity for placing such issues at the forefront of the legal debate.[44] Judy Scales-Trent found the support of white women crucial. The black faculty at her law school were not helpful, nor was the black faculty in the larger university community. She noted that a number of white men were supportive of her, but women tended to be more chummy, went to one another's homes for dinner, and did things together.[45] Annette Gordon-Reed noted that she received considerable support from white female colleagues as well. She also believed that black faculty have to be concerned about overextending themselves.[46]

Kimberlé Crenshaw found relationships with white women in the legal academy complex, but a sense of commonality existed. She argued that it is important for black women to use wisdom in deciding when to affirm these similarities, and to reject them when it is imperative to remind white women of the racial differences that exist. Crenshaw credited the strides in gender relations among black and white women to the emergence of critical legal studies, which subsequently developed into critical race theory. Sometimes having a common focus ends up creating allies out of people even though the issues they deem to be important are different. White women were able to create a discourse of opposition and to legitimize it so that women of color were able to concur with their arguments and, moreover, support some of the rhetoric that was being published although at times much of the rhetoric was misguided and fell short of accuracy.[47] Kimberly Jade Norwood argued that women of both races can be competitors or allies depending on the situation at hand.[48]

A number of these professors argue that irrationality occurs when the subject of race comes up for discussion. Moreover, they feel that when people discuss gender diversity, they are primarily referring to white women, and that those who are in the decision-making process do not stop to examine the comprehensive value system of the women they are bringing in. For many women, the only area in which they differ with their conservative male counterparts is their gender.[49]

Kimberlé Crenshaw elaborated on this point with her discussion of the relationships between black males and black females in the legal academy. Crenshaw argued that to the extent that black women can characterize their burden of being similar, there is lot of camaraderie and support. Where black women start to express their particular cut on their experiences in institutions, there is less support, particularly among senior black faculty. There is not a lot of expressed hostility, but rather there is a gender dimension to what black women faculty experience that requires a collective response.[50]

Crenshaw believed that the problem is larger than just gender. She saw it as problem that a group who is relatively new to the legal academy would encounter; however, she argued that mentoring is not a strong suit among a lot of African American academics. One has to become institutionally secure in order to be an effective mentor, and the majority of black academics do not feel as secure in this regard as their white counterparts. Part of the problem has to do with the asymmetry of the inference. When a white person mentors a white person, no one is standing around looking over their shoulder thinking "oh, this is preferential treatment," you are supporting this person because you share the same racial background. When people are free of such assumptions, they are much more able to perform a function for a colleague much more effectively, rather than being the subject of suspicion. When African Americans mentor one another, such concerns are always present.[51] Such assumptions are evident when tenure letters are written. There is a tendency to discount a reference if it comes from an African American faculty or to completely over interpret it when an African American says anything remotely critical. Thus, there is a discourse taking place that makes it difficult for mentoring to really happen in the same way.[52]

A small number of black faculty, according to Crenshaw, pride themselves on being one of the few or only. After having such a status, it is not that easy to suddenly turn around and be the person who is actively involved in developing the careers of young people. Most of these people are individuals who have been in white institutions for their entire careers and have been the only black faculty or one of two. Moreover, such strategies require you to think much more broadly, something that very few black faculty engage themselves in. Crenshaw felt that there is an identical racial hierarchy for both black and white women in the legal academy. There are more men at the top schools and more men in privileged positions, and more women at schools that are not seen in the same arena and more women who are in positions that are not full tenure-track or tenured positions. Thus, what may look like a gender issue may simply be a class issue among institutions or a generational issue because there are slightly more men than women in the older generation.[53]

Crenshaw believed that relationships between white men and black women are as complex in the academy as they are in society overall. In her estimation, there is the most distance between white males and African American women and the least amount of discursive overlap between projects with the two groups. From her own personal experience, Crenshaw, like Judy Scales-Trent, is pleased with the fact that she received a lot of feedback from white males as well as white females. Crenshaw stated that most of her colleagues of the first and second wave of black women law professors would be remiss if they did not acknowledge the fact that a number of white professors, particularly white males, read, critiqued, and applauded their work and wrote strong tenure letters on their behalf, as did a number of fellow black colleagues. She argued that such a situation is a boon and a bust, because it is good to be able to write across race and gender lines, but positive developments aside, power relationships in the academy still mean that even if you have ten African Americans read your work and like it, your committees are basically still going to look for what white faculty say.[54]

Unfortunately, committees are inclined to say that they do not want to reward scholarship that only appeals to such a small group. However, such comments are rarely made if the subfield in question is law and economics or jurisprudence. Crenshaw stated that she has yet to be asked to write a letter for a white male who writes in jurisprudence, but they are clearly going to be asked to write about her. Because of this dynamic, Crenshaw argued, one has to think about power by going outside of the individual relationships which are sometimes good and sometimes bad and look at the more structural institutional relationships. White faculty, particularly white male law faculty, are often afforded advantages that are not offered to faculty of color.

Joyce Hughes remembered a situation during the mid-1990s at Northwestern University School of Law where a white female colleague was denied tenure. Three people came up for tenure that year. They denied tenure to the woman and one of the white males and granted tenure to the other white male. The tenure and promotion committee were able to say that their decision was not sexist because they had denied tenure to a white man. The woman, who already had a tenure offer from another institution, packed up and left the university. The following year, tenure was revisited for the man who had been denied. The second time around, he was successful. It was possible that he was denied the previous year only because they did not want to provide the female candidate grounds for a sexual discrimination claim.[55]

During the academic year 1996–1997, Hughes relates, a senior tenured white woman joined the faculty and was dubbed "the new feminist." However, she stayed only one year. During the same year, an openly gay white woman arrived and faced a similar fate. These experiences made Hughes and her white female colleagues believe that their law school was rife with sexism. Several of the law professors believe that they must overcome the assumption that they are less qualified to teach than white men. One professor in particular who taught at an elite law school felt that she was not taken as seriously by the faculty due to the fact that she is a black woman. This same professor concluded that a number of white professors, particularly white men, enter with a presumption of intelligence that they deserve to be in the academy. She further argued that black men and women have to overcome the presumption that they are not "smart" and do not belong. Moreover, they have to overcome the presumption that issues of race are not central to legal scholarship and may not even be appropriate subjects for superior scholarship.

Taunya Lovell Banks described relationships between black and white women as an "uneasy tension." She recalled a conference that she, Paulette Caldwell, Patricia Williams, Regina Austin, and several other black women law professors attended. It was a meeting that white women had called to discuss the issues of hiring and retention of women and other hiring practices with various deans, provosts, and high-level university officials. The purpose of the meeting was to stress the need for hiring more females in the academy. According to Banks, throughout the meeting, there was token representation of women of color at best. They allowed only one black person to speak. Banks referred to it as a "white woman's show; however, they were making an attempt to demonstrate gender solidarity, so they kept talking about women and minorities." Banks said that she and her fellow black female colleagues were sitting in the back, saying, "Women and minorities, where are we?" It was clear that when these white women were talking about white women, they were referring to themselves, and when they were discussing minorities, they were discussing men of color. Women of color were once again marginalized or excluded from the conversation. Banks argued that this is a common complaint that many women of color have levied against white women, yet many white women refuse to address the issue or act oblivious to it.[56]

Banks recounted that when she was a new faculty member, one of her colleagues approached her and asked if she would be attending the meeting of women law professors from Virginia, Maryland, and the District of Columbia. Banks replied that she was unaware of such a meeting. Immediately afterward, the colleague approached the woman whose house the meeting was to take place in and asked why certain women (these were black women) would not be in attendance. According to Banks, the second woman looked sort of shamed faced and mumbled something incoherent. Suddenly, Banks herself started receiving looks from others around her. Such an incident made it clear to Banks that these women did not want her to be at that meeting, and she never bothered to attend. Another black woman who was hired for a permanent position encountered an identical experience.

Shortly afterward, Banks was seated at a table with the woman who had hosted the event and a black woman who had been visiting at another law school who was the speaker for this meeting. She had been invited by one of her white colleagues at the law school to attend the meeting. The white woman looked at Banks's colleague and asked her why she did not attend. Banks asked why she had not invited her. The woman became defensive and voiced assumptions that this black woman would not want to travel such a long commute, not mentioning the fact that she had invited a white woman who was not even part of the faculty who also lived in Baltimore. Banks suggested that her colleague include the other woman of color's name on the list and let her decide whether she would attend. The woman hesitated. The conversation confirmed to Banks that this was another deliberate calculation to exclude a woman of color from an event.

Because of such common incidents, Banks harbors no illusion that there is any sort of sisterhood among black and white women at her law school, and she has made clear to the majority of her white female colleagues that when they are talking about sisterhood, they are talking about white sisterhood. Interestingly, Banks says that despite the lack of camaraderie among black and white women, she did receive a huge boost in the legal academy because of a white woman, fellow black women, and one male of color who was not black. These individuals were among her greatest supporters. Her belief is that if any person of color is going to coalesce or align themselves with white women, they need to understand why they are doing so and be aware of the reasons that white women have for aligning themselves with a person of color. More importantly, she believed it is imperative for black women to be aware that those alliances are going to be temporary (usually to do battle against white men), yet it does not mean that all white females are to be distrusted.[57]

Beverly Moran largely concurred with Banks that relationships between black and white women are fair to poor in the legal academy.[58] The late self-described "black, lesbian, feminist poet" Audre Lorde, who died of cancer in 1992, discussed the issue of white female periodic opportunism and arrogance in her classic 1984 book, *Sister Outsider*.

> Today, with the defeat of ERA, the tightening economy, and increased conservatism, it is easier once again for white women to believe the dangerous fantasy that if you are good enough, pretty enough, sweet enough, quiet enough, teach the children to behave, hate the right people, and marry the right men, then you will be allowed to co-exist with patriarchy in relative peace, at least until a man needs your job or until the neighborhood rapist comes along. And true, unless one lives and loves in the trenches it is difficult to remember that the war against dehumanization is ceaseless.[59]

Banks also discovered problems among black women in the legal academy. She believed that more than a few black women internalize the hatred that the larger society directs toward them and, in turn, disperse it out to one another. She argued that despite such conflicts, she has had an extremely rewarding experience being a member of the Northeast Corridor Collective, a group of black women law professors who teach at law schools in the northeast and meet several times per year as a support group for one another.[60] On the contrary, Dorothy Roberts believed that black women in the legal academy have a very strong relationship in that whenever they meet, they share stories and give advice about dealing with disrespectful students. According to Roberts, they support one another in scholastic and other academic matters as well as in one another's personal lives.[61]

Taunya Lovell Banks believed that southern law schools are more comfortable hiring African Americans as opposed to other minorities.[62] This is probably rooted in the historical fact that there is more familiarity with blacks as opposed to Latinos, Asians, Indians, Arabs, and other people of color. Dorothy Roberts largely confirmed this belief. She stated that she saw more barriers to Asians and Latinos entering the legal academy. Despite the stereotype of Asians being the "model minority" and comprising the highest percentage of students of color at many law schools, they are not hired at comparable rates. Roberts concluded that this could very well have to do with the fact that whites harbor some degree of discomfort with having Asian faculty as colleagues.[63]

In her 1995 book *The Rooster's Egg: On the Persistence of Prejudice*, law professor Patricia Williams commented on her experiences with racism and sexism in the legal academy:

> I have been associated with at least five universities since then, and at every one I was the first Black or only Black, or the first Black woman ever hired. In each job I have had, there has been some moment where I have protested what I perceived to be some thoughtless or intentional form of bias. And my reputation for either remarkable insight or radical troublemaking has grown accordingly.[64]

All the women interviewed state that diversity exists among black faculty. Anita Allen argued that you have black faculty of various political and ideological perspectives—liberals, conservatives, Marxists, nationalists, progressives, Afrocentrists, and so on. Because of this, you have arguments and various debates and controversies at almost every law school. However, it is a healthy diversity to have pluralism among black colleagues.[65] Joyce Hughes has a more restrictive view of race:

> I believe that it is easier for black faculty to have good relationships with white faculty to the extent that white faculty perceive that one is—and the black person's self-perception is—Afro-Saxon. If there actually is no difference, all black faculty have to worry about is having the white faculty get over the color barrier. And as soon as the white faculty get over the color barrier, if the black person's thoughts and perceptions about the world are exactly the same as whites, then they get along fine.[66]

Both Joyce Hughes and Taunya Lovell Banks encountered hostility from certain black males as law students. Both women concurred that sexism in their respective law schools was endemic. There was an attitude that any woman who was in law school was taking the position of a male and that jobs that were sometimes awarded to women should be reserved for black men. Many black male faculty subscribed to this mindset.[67] Both Beverly Moran and Kimberly Jade Norwood echoed similar sentiments. They envision the relationships between black men and women in the legal academy as complex, ranging from poor at times to excellent at other times.[68]

Banks recalled the experience of a fellow black student who came up to her and another black female law student, shook his finger in their faces, and remarked, "Because of you two ladies, two good black men are dying in Vietnam." Given the fact that Banks had attended Syracuse University as an undergraduate and had encountered racist behavior from whites who did not want to be her roommate, coupled with hostile behavior from a few faculty at the institution, she had acquired a more detached attitude than her colleague who had attended Fisk University. Because her colleague had attended a historically black institution which prided itself on uplifting black people and was a Phi Beta Kappa, she was unprepared for the disparaging comments she received from fellow blacks. Banks felt that this was a factor in her friend's performing at a lower rate than she probably should have. Banks, who had managed to create a tough exterior, was able to combat or dismiss such behavior more easily.[69] Dorothy Roberts believed, however, that in the overwhelming majority of cases, black men and women in general have a good relationship with one another.[70]

In regard to race, a few of the law professors argued that law schools are bastions of political correctness. There are things that you cannot say or do. But there are institutional issues about faculty. Annette Gordon-Reed mentioned a young mother trying to go through the tenure process and the kinds of requirements she faced that were not part of the process when older white male scholars were going up for the same level of job security. Gordon-Reed cited an example of a prestigious law school where a law professor had to have three articles published in the first six years. She argued that these are the kinds of rules that place young women at a disadvantage. It is a choice of having children or not having children.[71]

A number of institutional issues have not been addressed in a systematic and good fashion in the academy between men and women and how they are groomed for tenure.[72] Aside from this situation, a number of the women professors interviewed state that they have served as mentors for or have been mentored by black males. A primary complaint is that the number of black faculty in the legal academy is so small that it results in isolation. This is the major complaint of many professors interviewed. A number of the professors interviewed share the same story of entering a room and often being the only person of color there. One professor remarked that it is usually just a momentary thing, not the sort of thing that leaves you permanently depressed, but it makes you wonder how whites would respond if the situation were reversed. They would probably not be there, because the majority of whites, including the most liberal ones, would not subject themselves to being in an awkward situation. Many blacks, however, are called upon to subject themselves to such situations on a regular basis.[73]

Trying to educate whites about race is a great risk for people of color. They risk not only that whites will not care and will prefer to perpetuate the status quo, but also that even caring whites will not hear or understand the pain of racism. Talking about racism and white supremacy is painful for whites as well, but in a different way. Whites must confront their role as oppressors, or at least as beneficiaries of the racial oppression of others, in a race-based hierarchy. The pain of oppression must be communicated to the dominant group if there is to be any understanding of the effects of racism and white supremacy. This act of sharing, however, contains the risk that the pain of oppression will be appropriated by the dominant group for its own purpose. It would be difficult and to some degree unfair to lay all the blame at the feet of the legal academy; rather, it is primarily the situation of the demographics. However, many of these professors make clear that they often longed for an idealistic situation where things would be 50/50 or even greater, where the possibility of your perspectives would be much more represented. You would have people who would be much more attuned to the experiences of people of color and thus act accordingly.[74]

Several of the law professors believed that for every step forward, there is some price to be paid. For many of the women of this generation who entered the legal academy in the 1970s and 1980s, they quickly became aware that they had to establish a tough exterior in an effort to survive. In this sense, they were certainly strengthened; but many argued that such strength came at a price, and that price was full individuality. So much of their energy was put into survival and protection against warfare that, at times, it became very difficult to fully realize themselves as individuals.[75]

All of the professors interviewed stated that they found racism as prevalent among liberals law professors as they did among conservatives. They felt that academia is more racist and elitist than other institutions due to the fact that there is a considerable economic advantage or profit motive inside academic institutions. But for the most part, the capital, the currency, is different. Thus, there is a strong likelihood that there is a more virulent form of racism inside the legal academy as opposed to outside of it.[76]

All of the women interviewed saw racism and sexism in the legal academy as intersected. The manner in which the two are expressed in the academy affects those who are members of it differently than it does those who are members of other institutions.[77] Despite what many of these women credit as progress, they are quick to point out that subtle and overt forms of sexism remain alive and well in the academy. When the number of female law students began to equal and in some cases surpass the number of males, law schools were hard pressed not to hire women for their faculty. This evolution has come slowly but surely. Even today, many of the professors interviewed argue that there is still not a critical mass of women faculty in any legal institution, and where women are members of faculty, they often do not have the same status or privileges, and they are not treated in the same manner as men on the faculty. However, the tremendous public relations problems that law schools encountered due to the severe dearth of women on their faculties has forced them to address the issue of gender inequity in addition to the issues that face women of color. The unyielding issues of equal pay, sexism, racism, and particularly affirmative action will be the topic of discussion in the next chapter.

Notes

1. Stephanie M. Wildman and Trina Grillo, *Privilege Revealed: How Invisible Preference Undermines America* (New York: New York University Press, 1996), 103–7.

2. bell hooks, "Overcoming White Supremacy: A Comment," in *Talking Back: Thinking Feminist, Thinking Black* (Boston: South End, 1989), 112–13.

3. Wildman and Grillo, *Privilege Revealed*, 103–10.

4. These factors were perennial issues in the life of every professor I interviewed.

5. Wildman and Grillo, *Privilege Revealed*, 103–10.

6. Angela Harris, "Race and Essentialism in Feminist Legal Theory," *Stanford Law Review* 42 (1990): 588.

7. Gloria T. Hull and Barbara Smith, "Introduction: The Politics of Black Women's Studies," in *All the Women Are White, All the Men Are Black, but Some of Us Are Brave*, ed. Gloria T. Hull, Patricia Bell Scott, and Barbara Smith (New York: Feminist Press, 1982).

8. Harris, "Race and Essentialism," 601.

9. The overwhelming majority of law professors I interviewed stated that their presence in a position of authority in the classroom made more than a few whites (particularly white males) very uncomfortable.

10. Wildman and Grillo, *Privilege Revealed*, 124–31.

11. Wildman and Grillo, *Privilege Revealed*, 124–31.

12. Wildman and Grillo, *Privilege Revealed*, 124–31.

13. Angela Harris writes, "In this society, it is only white people who have the luxury of 'having no color'; only white people have been able to imagine that sexism and racism are separate experiences." Harris, "Race and Essentialism," 604. Harris also describes a meeting of women law professors who were asked to pick out two or three words to describe who they were. Harris reports that none of the white women mentioned race; all of the women of color did.

14. Interview with Paulette Caldwell, March 26, 1997; interview with Kimberlé Crenshaw, March 11, 1999; interview with Judy Scales-Trent, February 19, 1997.

15. bell hooks, "Overcoming White Supremacy," 112; Wildman and Grillo, *Privilege Revealed*, 123–30.

16. Kimberlé Crenshaw, "Demarginalizing the Intersection of Race and Sex: A Black Feminist Critique of Antidiscrimination Doctrine, Feminist Theory, and Antiracist Politics," *University of Chicago Legal Forum* (1989), 139; Harris, "Race and Essentialism," 581.

17. Interview with Taunya Lovell Banks, March 18, 1998.

18. Wildman and Grillo, *Privilege Revealed*, 90–98.

19. Interview with Anita Allen, February 24, 1997.

20. Scales-Trent interview.

21. Scales-Trent interview.

22. This was virtually the unanimous assumption from every law professor interviewed.

23. Pauli Murray, "The Liberation of Black Women," in *Voices of the New Feminism*, ed. Mary Lou Thompson (Boston: Beacon, 1970), 87–105.

24. Crenshaw interview.

25. Banks interview; Caldwell interview; Crenshaw interview; Trent interview.

26. Interview with Annette Gordon-Reed, January 5, 2001; Banks interview; Crenshaw interview.

27. Gordon-Reed interview; Banks interview; Crenshaw interview.

28. Lani Guinier, Michelle Fine, and Jane Balin, *Becoming Gentlemen: Women, Law School, and Institutional Change* (Boston: Beacon, 1997).

29. Interview with Lani Guinier, May 15, 1997.

30. Scales-Trent interview.

31. Judy Scales-Trent, "Commonalities: On Being Black and White, Different and the Same," *Yale Journal of Law and Feminism* 2 (1990): 305, 322–24.

32. Scales-Trent interview.

33. Allen interview; interview with Kimberly Jade Norwood, August 19, 2007.

34. Allen interview.

35. Gordon-Reed interview; Banks interview; Allen interview.

36. *Brown v. Board of Education of Topeka, Kansas*, 347 U.S. (1954).

37. Allen interview.

38. Allen interview.

39. Scales-Trent interview.

40. Patricia J. Williams, *The Rooster's Egg: On the Persistence of Prejudice* (Cambridge, MA: Harvard University Press, 1995), 90.

41. Anita Hill, *Speaking Truth to Power* (New York: Doubleday, 1997), 49.

42. Allen interview.

43. Interview with Dorothy Roberts, September 20, 2007.

44. Allen interview.

45. Scales-Trent interview.

46. Gordon-Reed interview.

47. Crenshaw interview.

48. Interview with Kimberly Jade Norwood, August 19, 2007.

49. Norwood interview.

50. Crenshaw interview.

51. Crenshaw interview.

52. Banks interview; Caldwell interview; Crenshaw interview; Gordon-Reed interview; Hughes interview.

53. Crenshaw interview.

54. Crenshaw interview.

55. Hughes interview.

56. Banks interview.

57. Banks interview.

58. Interview with Beverly Moran, September 5, 2007.

59. Audre Lorde, *Sister Outsider: Essays and Speeches* (Freedom, CA: Crossing, 1984), 119.

60 Banks interview.

61. Roberts interview.

52. Banks interview.

63. Roberts interview.

64. Williams, *The Rooster's Egg*, 93.

65. Allen interview.

66. Hughes interview.

67. Banks interview; Hughes interview.

68. Moran interview; Norwood interview.

69. Banks interview.

70. Roberts interview.

71. Gordon-Reed interview.

72. This was the general consensus of all the law professors interviewed.

73. Gordon-Reed interview.

74. Crenshaw interview; Gordon-Reed interview.

75. Banks interview; Hughes interview; Scales-Trent interview.

76. Banks interview; Norwood interview.

77. This was the consensus of every professor interviewed.

CHAPTER FOUR

~

Affirmative Action: Combating Assumptions

The desire that we live in a pluralistic society of equality has been a utopian ideal echoed by many over the decades. Legal scholar Stephanie Wildman argued that such a vision has undergone a significant number of transformations over the years: it was originally referred to as "integration,"[1] then "affirmative action," and then "diversity" and "multiculturalism."[2] Over time, each of the terms garnered negative perceptions from right-wing, reactionary conservatives, and a new phrase had to be implemented to keep King's vision moving forward. Despite progress, white males still predominate in many areas where the status quo is relevant. One institution where the dream of integration has failed to reach fruition is the legal academy.[3] This chapter focuses on legal education in the context of affirmative action and examines integration, gender inequity, fairness, and exclusion as well as how these factors manifest themselves within the legal academy.

The legal academy is the primary route to gaining access to the legal profession.[4] Even in the early twenty-first century, the academy and the profession remain primarily white and male, and those who are maintaining the status quo are the white males who dominate the legal academy.[5] This represents a problem on several fronts. The white males who dominate the legal academy are likely to have come of age during the era when Jim Crow, legal segregation, discrimination, and other injustices were beginning to diminish; however, more often than not, these are people who were influenced by such policies and thus are more inclined to adopt the mentality that accompanies such retrograde ideas. They grew up with the assumption that "white is

93

right," that blacks are "intellectually inferior," and that women are not much better than blacks.[6] Moreover, rather than embrace diversity and ethnic pluralism, these individuals are more likely to see these as insignificant nuisances that result in more harm rather than good, in that they force those in the legal academy to reexamine their value systems.[7]

In interviews, several legal scholars made it evident that attempts to aggressively integrate the legal academy are more likely to be met with resistance rather than cooperation.[8] Other legal scholars argue that less litigious approaches through voluntary action can be effective.[9] Association of American Law Schools (AALS) President Herma Hill Kay noted that three past AALS presidents stressed the importance and value to legal education of the commitment to achieving progress in recruiting and retaining professors who are people of color, women, gay, or lesbian. Professor Kay also made clear that members of the aforementioned groups have been the victims of historical discrimination and are just recently entering a profession that has always been overrepresented by white males. Kay stated that it is imperative that the voices of those groups which have been either isolated or marginalized for decades be acknowledged and given respect by those in the dominant group. This, according to Kay, is the only effective way for diversity to succeed in the legal academy.[10]

When law schools decide to hire a candidate, his or her qualifications are almost always at the top of the discussion. While it is understandable that no one would want to hire an unqualified person, more often than not, the definition of qualification takes on different meanings for different people. For many white faculty, particularly white male faculty, the issue of qualifications becomes secondary to other factors such as collegiality, pedigree, and comfort level. In short, a candidate who exhibits qualities similar to mine is the sort of person I want to work with.[11]

Taunya Lovell Banks and Anita Allen found that whites are comfortable with blacks and other minorities in token numbers. Banks believed there is a psychological demand to have at least one or two black professors on the faculty. Like Banks, Allen argued that there is a psychological need to have at least one or two blacks in the vicinity to assuage any level of guilt or denial, but beyond that, no more if at all possible.[12] In her book *Privilege Revealed: How Invisible Preference Undermine America*, Stephanie Wildman discussed the argument that renowned legal scholar Derrick Bell described as the "tipping point issue." Like his black female cohorts, Bell argued that for whites, a small number of blacks and other people of color is acceptable; moreover, it is important that they be "the right type" of minority: a safe person who does not make any waves, knows his or her place, and will not disrupt the "good ol' boy" network. Any person who can adhere to these rules is acceptable; those who refuse to conform to the mores set forth by the rigid world of the legal academy are not acceptable.[13]

Given that white males have dominated the environment of the legal academy for so long, many of them are unable or unwilling to relinquish any power, both literally and psychologically. Many white males, particularly conservative ones, have made a committed effort to retain what they see as their divine right to maintain control and power in the legal academy. More than a few of them believe that their vision of the world is the appropriate one. However, many women and legal scholars of color argue that incorporating a plethora of perspectives would provide a certain degree of equality to the legal academy.[14]

A number of the professors interviewed for this book argued that the problem with affirmative action is often one of language. They believe that how the policy is explained to the larger public is often complex. Law professors like Kimberly Jade Norwood and Dorothy Roberts believe it is imperative that the public be aware of benefits that affirmative action provides to the larger society.[15] In fact, all of the women interviewed believe that affirmative action is integral to the betterment of American society.

Many of these women believe that it is crucial to examine how the term is employed in society at any given time. All of them state that affirmative action helped them land their first jobs in the legal profession and gave them considerable advantages in several key positions that they obtained throughout their careers. Some go even further and say that they would not have had the careers or the level of success that they achieved had it not been for affirmative action.[16]

Several of the law professors mentioned that they were the products of historically black colleges or universities (HBCUs). They are quick to mention that during their tenure as students, a number of white students were their cohorts at these institutions. Moreover, they mentioned that these students were the products of affirmative action whether wittingly or unwittingly. All the women interviewed concur that women and minorities have benefited considerably from affirmative action. In fact, the biggest beneficiaries of affirmative action are white females.

All of the professors interviewed believed it is imperative to combat the commonly held notion that merit equals whiteness and maleness. Until whites and blacks (and all other groups of color) have had the opportunity to work together, and until people of color have obtained positions of power, we need some form of affirmative action, some way to change the mindset that has existed in this country for four hundred years. Merit becomes the red herring when one is talking about the admission of people of color, and there is an assumption that merit is always absent in people of color and women, and somehow mysteriously present in white males.[17]

Some of the law professors interviewed argued that the idea of affirmative action came about in the late 1960s and early 1970s as a compromise between established forces in the society and disadvantaged groups, such as people of color and women. History has been lost on many people who are unaware of the dire situation that many women and people of color endured. The view held among many people of color and women was that Title VII and other aspects of the Civil Rights Act of 1964 would not dismantle discrimination fast enough.

A number of people believe that affirmative action came about as a result of the urban riots that took place in many of our nation's cities in the late 1960s. Indeed, the phrase "Burn, baby, burn" quickly became apparent to the powers that be. They realized something had better be done to address the chronic economic inequality that was rampant in many of our nation's inner cities. The slow but gradual method of gaining equality through the judicial system was not moving with the speed that many felt was necessary to address such societal woes. To these individuals, rapid change had to occur.

Legal scholar Patricia Williams stated:

In 1975 I had already exceeded my parents' wildest dreams. I was Black, Black was beautiful, and I was graduating from law school, any law school, never mind that it was Harvard. The World had turned upside down in terms of what any of us had ever dared hope was possible, and things would never be the same again.[18]

Anita Hill described her view on affirmative action in these terms:

Fortunately, I grew up during a time when social forces were such that I might have a better opportunity to realize my family's and my own expectations. In ways small and large, from school lunch programs to student grants and loans, they enhanced my opportunities for a better life than the one enjoyed by my parents and grandparents. I no doubt have benefited from affirmative action programs, which looked at my race, gender, and background and determined whether I would be admitted. But I am not ashamed of this fact, nor do I apologize for it. Such programs provided me with the opportunity to prove myself, no more, no less. After admission, my success or failure would be determined by my efforts. I do not consider myself either more or less worthy than my colleagues in the same program.[19]

The myth of minority incompetence is commonplace in the legal academy. There is often a perception that if a woman or person of color (with the possible exceptions of Asians) receives a prestigious position, then the standards were lowered. This perception is not limited to white faculty; some students, including students of color, harbor this belief. These incidents have more to do with what one professor refers to as "frivolous society people," some ultraconservative students who have been nurtured throughout and are angry. More often than not, they are the angry children of angry white people of the preceding generation.[20] As one black female law professor stated:

> Allan Bakke filed the first reverse discrimination suit, against the University of California, during my entering year, and it was bitterly controversial. My professors were constantly cited in the newspapers, some complaining about how Blacks were displacing more productive White men, some damning us with faint praise saying it was necessary to give the Blacks—God-Bless-Them—their day in court too. It was revealed to the press that Harvard's admissions process was done in two tiers, one for Blacks, one for Whites, the average Black scores being lower that the average White scores. What they didn't mention was that Harvard's admissions process had lots of tiers, such as the one for children of alumni, who were admitted at rates grossly, even obscenely disproportionate to the "scored" worth. Harvard had tiers for women, tiers for veterans, tiers that for whatever reason admitted some good, smart White men with scores far *lower* than those of any good, smart Black students. But the public controversy was never that nuanced.[21]

Some people believed that integration limited their options. Because of this, they instilled in their children a false belief that their futures were being jeopardized because colleges and universities were admitting more minorities, people of color, and women. As many of the black women law professors are aware, some students are angry, thinking that something they were entitled to (especially if they are legacies) had been taken away from them, and they were never forced by their law school or professors to question whether they were entitled to that. As a consequence, women and people of color who have forced them to question this have become the targets of white male rage. For these people, it is the natural order that whites, especially men, should be granted preference. It is their perception that it is whites who primarily support the institution, and the preference is of quid pro quo in the institution, a historical intertwining of life in the institution with the life of families who have produced alumni. They have a story which naturalized all of this, and they cannot expand it to include other groups. It is a denial and resistance to history. Taunya Lovell Banks argued that whites in this country do not have to think about entitlement. It is part of their culture and white transparency.

Class distinction and resentment are also prevalent regarding the issue of affirmative action. As one law professor who was the product of a middle-class background stated:

> What I achieved is undoubtedly the result of my having been among the first generation of affirmative action babies. I know that there are those who would begrudge me this sense of contented accomplishment—as though I was not deserving of affirmative action and should have just ignored any other kind of limitation in my life. It's the Oliver Twistian advice given frequently to Blacks deemed middle class: be grateful for the gruel because children are starving in the inner cities. . . . I do not feel apologetic in the slightest for having transgressed at every step of the way the demographic expectations for my "place" or my "type" as female and as Black.[22]

Those of us on the outside saw a number of privileges and advantages accorded the white male majority: all white schools or heavily male law schools that meant affirmative action for men and white men; alumni preferences, especially at the elite universities, that meant affirmative action for men by and large and were never thought of as affirmative action; subsidies to farmers who are paid not to grow certain crops; subsidies to businesses; and tax forgiveness. There are various forms of affirmative action, but the issue has been crafted by its opponents in a way to denigrate black people. Even though white women have been the biggest beneficiaries, many of the attacks on affirmative action are couched in terms of black people, and increasingly Latinos. Legal scholar Cheryl Harris, the author of a scholarly article on whiteness as property, challenges the legal academy to reexamine the concept of white skin privilege.[23]

In her profound 1995 study on prejudice, *The Rooster's Egg*, legal scholar Patricia Williams, professor of law at Columbia University, stated:

> White students had no hesitation about asking Black students what their LSAT scores had been in very aggressive demonstrations of their disdain for our presence. And when racial woes intersected with gender miseries, you had such low moments as when some Black male law students announced that they were not interested in dating Black female law students, but were looking for "the more feminine" types, of whom there were rumored to be an abundance at Lesley Junior College just down the road.[24]

Annette Gordon-Reed concurred that affirmative action is a hotly debated issue in the legal academy and argued that there is a misguided belief among many whites (especially men) that, if you are black, all you have to do is show up to places and you are going to receive a job. She recounted a

situation where a black candidate had just given a talk, and a white male colleague of hers commented, "Well, he's the right color, you know," under his
breath.[25]

As the only black law professor at the law school at the time, such a reaction was disturbing to Gordon-Reed. It reconfirmed to her the belief of many
whites that black candidates are able to waltz into positions with minimal
qualifications and without having to compete. Gordon-Reed disputed the
notion held by many whites that affirmative action has resulted in a plethora
of people of color swarming like locusts throughout the legal academy. The
numbers, she argued, tell a different story. According to Gordon-Reed, law
schools are looking for people from a certain school, a certain profile, and it
is this sort of restrictive criteria that keeps the numbers of minorities low.
Gordon-Reed argued that there is considerable lip service given to affirmative action, but the level of commitment dedicated to it is more questionable.[26]

As Patricia Williams noted:

> Law school, with its frenetic corporate competitiveness, is to some degree mis-
> erable for all who enter its portals, regardless of race and gender. At the same
> time, I think the new presence of Black and female students provided fresh
> meat for the old cruel hazing games that labeled and marked the "mental veg-
> etarians" separating them from the ones who knew how to tear a carcass limb
> from limb. Racism ands sexism were passed off as just "practical jokes," just a
> device to see who was fittest to survive, just a little collegial jockeying for po-
> sition, just a test for admission to the inner circles of some ultimate game of
> the then-popular Dungeons and Dragons.[27]

Anita Allen took Gordon-Reed's and Williams's arguments one step further,
saying that many people believe that black people belong at the bottom of
the totem pole, and that any system backed by government that challenges
or threatens the idea that blacks belong on the bottom is going to be resented
by everyone else. Many people genuinely believe that blacks are seldom the
best-qualified candidate for a position.[28]

In her book *Notes of a White, Black Woman*, Judy Scales-Trent discussed
the issue of affirmative action and qualifications and stigma. At SUNY-
Buffalo School of Law, as she was beginning to become more acquainted with
the tenure struggle, a white male colleague had just been denied tenure. He
came into her office soon afterward to offer advice about tenure and to share
the lessons learned from his loss. He told her the pace of publishing was important, that he waited too long to publish his first piece, and that as a result,
his colleagues lost confidence in him as a scholar. He made it clear to her

that it was imperative that she publish early. Scales-Trent appreciated that a colleague who was obviously experiencing some disappointment would give sagacious advice to a colleague who was a novice. The colleague provided her with more suggestions and then concluded, "But really, you don't need to worry, because you're Black. You will get tenure anyhow."[29]

Scales-Trent stated that his comment hit her like a smack across the face. She suddenly became incensed that he invalidated all her past and future work so readily. She responded that if her tenure was such a "sure thing," then why had none of the black law professors who had arrived here before she did receive tenure. To her soon to be departed colleague, the facts were irrelevant. In his eyes, her work would not be judged on its merit. Moreover, he seemed to think he was denied tenure not only because of his publication record but because he was white. The only reason she would be granted tenure was because she was black. Scales-Trent believed that affirmative action is frequently used as a tool by those who feel threatened and weak to attack those who are vulnerable. She argued that it was a convenient, ever present weapon that could be used against an ever present victim.[30]

Patricia Williams recalled experiences she encountered serving on admissions committees:

> Sitting on university admissions committees, for example, I have seen Black candidates who write on their applications comments such as, "Don't admit me if you have to lower your standards." I have never seen the same acutely self-conscious disavowals from students who are admitted because they meet some geographical criterion—such as living in Wyoming, or France, or some other underrepresented area—or who are older reentry students, or football heroes, or alumni children. I think this is so because these latter inclusionary categories are thought to indicate group life experiences, whether we call them cultures or not, that "enrich" rather than "lower."[31]

She further argued:

> The question then becomes not how to undo inclusionary affirmative action programs, but how to undo the stigma of inferiority that not merely resides in the label or designation of race, but that according to our national symbology, is actually *embodied* in Black presence. If eliminating the stigma were truly as simple as erasing labels then perhaps enough White-Out in our cases and codes would eliminate the problem once and for all. But it is the ferocious mythology of blackness (or otherness) as the embodiment of inferiority that persists whether Blacks are inside or outside particular institutions and regardless of how they perform.[32]

Lani Guinier argued that the issue of affirmative action has been depicted in polarizing terms with no meaningful level of analysis given to the policy. She believed that the American public would be much less hostile to affirmative action if the discussions on the issue were similar to those of jury deliberations for court cases. The first thing they do is deliver a straw vote. The jury is much less likely to render a unanimous verdict in a relatively short period of time. Whereas if they go around the room and, instead of asking people to vote, they ask them for their views and to recollect facts, the jury is much more likely to have an accurate recollection of the facts as people pool their knowledge. Once all the facts are placed before the jury, the jury is much more likely to come to a consensus sooner, and the people who participate in these juries report a higher degree of satisfaction with the process.[33]

Dorothy Roberts concurred that more analysis is needed. She argued that it is important to focus on the different ways that the legal academy measures merit, how it comprises a diverse community, and the extent to which they want the legal academy to reflect society so that people can be prepared to assume leadership positions in society.[34]

Guinier mentioned the case of Cheryl Hopwood, a white woman who applied to the University of Texas Law School but was not accepted. Her index score was higher than sixty-three of the ninety-two black and Chicano students who applied and were accepted. But her index score was also higher than about 140 white students who applied and were accepted. However, she looked at the black and Chicano students as the people who took her place, as opposed to the white students who also scored lower than she did on this index. What happened, according to Guinier, was that she had points taken off her index because she had attended a state and a community college. What this suggested, according to Guinier, is that there is rampant class bias in the admission system that many people do not discuss. Rather than examine these factors, people identify black or Chicano students due to their visibility. It is a form of scapegoating. It is a way of distracting people from examining the real problem, which is that there are too few places and too many people applying for them, and as a society we have not done enough to open up opportunities to higher education to all of the people who are able to take advantage of it. It is a way of avoiding the real conversation that Americans need to have about the distribution of resources in society.[35]

Dorothy Roberts echoed Guinier's sentiments; however, she believed that there is a more direct, bigoted motivation behind the more recent attacks on affirmative action. She argues that such attacks are being levied by the conservative political right and other conservatives in an effort to reinforce white privilege. Roberts further argued that there has to be a concerted commitment to increasing the numbers of students and faculty of color in order to overcome the retrograde presumption that blacks, Latinos, other minorities, and in some cases women do not belong in the academy.[36]

Kimberlé Crenshaw argued that those who have called for the elimination of affirmative action because they see it as a form of preferential treatment based on race are hypocritical. A number of other groups have lobbied for explicit policies in an effort to protect their interests. However, affirmative action as it applies to people of color is the one thing that is taken out of the equation, and that analysis is apparent not only in traditional affirmative action but in many other arenas. A good comparison for this, Crenshaw argued, would be voter rights. One can draw congressional districts to protect the interests of Republicans or Democrats, for example, and any number of groups can be furthered through their ability to get into the political process and work the system in order to get something for their benefit. The groups that have had their hands tied are African Americans, Latinos, and Asians in California. It is difficult to look at such a situation and argue that color blindness is at work. If anything, it is color consciousness of a certain kind.[37]

When a district is drawn in a way that maximizes the potential of people of color to elect someone of their choice, that is seen as unconstitutional. If the group whose interests are furthered are referred to as Democrats or Republicans, then that is okay. So there is discrimination playing out in the selective way in which certain things are seen as illegitimate preferences and others are seen as reasonable public policy. Another factor is the hidden dimension, the relationship between the preferences that operate in favor of privilege and power and how that makes it necessary to have policies to deal with the differential consequences of that on people of color. Crenshaw discussed the examples of *Shaw v. Reno* and *Miller v. Johnson*,[38] where districts were very misshaped in order to protect incumbents. So you have a policy that allows legislatures to draw districts in a manner that protects certain interests. African Americans are not drawn into districts that allow them to elect someone of their choice, but another district is drawn that allows white people to get what they want.[39]

A parallel exists in admissions to ivy-league institutions, where many whites believe that the only people benefiting from affirmative action are people of color; in fact, most studies indicate that the children of alumni have a far better chance of gaining admission. This is another situation where privilege incumbency gives you preferences, and it tends to be okay with society. In fact, 90 percent of living ivy-league alums are white people. Many do not recognize that ivy-league schools have a history of not shaping their institutions to further the educational needs and interests of the community. There has been a last-ditch effort by whites to say, "Oh, by the way, we'll let a few of you in." However, maintaining this privilege of incumbency is unconstitutional.[40]

Many Americans have failed to comprehend the whole debate about what is preference and what is not. The things that benefit traditionally excluded groups strike people as more of a departure from what is normal or normative, and privileges go in the direction that they have always gone in. This is somewhat reminiscent of forty acres and a mule, where the argument was that you can't give those people anything because it will encourage them to be indolent. A pivotal reality gets constructed that continues to privilege how power usually functions, and that makes it questionable or unconstitutional to intervene in a way that disempowerment actually happens. Crenshaw is a member of an institution where affirmative action was created as a political issue and then became a factor inside the institution that students fought and debated.[41]

Roberts and several other professors interviewed believe that the attacks on affirmative action have been politically motivated, and that any hiring that takes place is often done reluctantly. Taunya Lovell Banks went one step further and argued that unless there is a significant change in attitude from powerful agencies in America, we will continue to see more isolated forms of affirmative action. She believed that law schools will realize that it is good business to have a racially and gender diverse student body and faculty.[42] While every woman interviewed is a fervent supporter of affirmative action, they caution that it is important that minority groups take advantage of the policy for progressive reasons, as opposed to retrograde ones, such as getting into battles where there is ultimately no victor.

Many scholars of color from various professions adamantly state that it is imperative that institutions of higher education aggressively practice the policy of affirmative action in an effort to reflect the ideals of equality, fairness, and equal opportunity that are supposed to be the representative hallmarks of our culture. As legal scholar Stephanie Wildman argued, "without affirmative action, we cannot ensure that our institutions reflect the ideals of equality, fairness, and equal opportunity that are part of our culture. Law professors are not unique in this society in holding divergent views about affirmative action. Law schools, as institutions composed of the individuals within them, also are not unique in society as places where the dominant cultural majority remains in control. Law schools, like other societal institutions, are composed of well-intentioned individuals, who, for the most part, genuinely want to be free of discriminatory attitudes."[43]

Opponents of affirmative action argue that the policy fails to recognize merit; it promotes supposedly "unqualified" people, amounts to reverse discrimination, and unfairly pegs those who benefit from it with the stigma of inferiority.[44] Yet much of the time, the issue of merit is a fallacy. Numerous whites (particularly white men) have been afforded satisfying, well-paying jobs due to the fact that they are white, male, and had the correct connections.[45] More than half of all the desired jobs in America are held by people who knew someone. The majority of people that have these connections are white. In regard to the discrimination argument, there is no such thing as "reverse discrimination." The fact is that all laws discriminate to some extent. Whites who argue that affirmative action penalizes those who had nothing to do with past discrimination fail to realize that history has afforded whites advantages that many still are benefiting from today. Affirmative action does not take away their advantages; if anything, it makes a salutatory effort to address past and (in some cases, contemporary) injustices that have been perpetrated on minorities and women.

Interestingly, many whites and some blacks, mainly black conservatives, argue that affirmative action stigmatizes blacks who benefit from it, burdening them with feelings of inferiority. This is a dubious argument at best. Many groups of Americans are the beneficiaries of affirmative action—veterans, the disabled, people from certain regions of the nation, women, and so on. Yet few argue that these groups are filled with "self-doubt," "feelings of inferiority," and other psychological maladies that supposedly accompany those who are the beneficiaries of this policy. The reality is that the group that benefits the most from affirmative action is not black people; it is white women.[46]

"Unqualified" has been a label that people of color, and to a lesser degree women, have had to deal with throughout history. More than a few whites have negative stereotypes about blacks and other minorities. Such retrograde ideas, fears, suspicions, and other emotions have been deeply ingrained in the white American psyche for centuries. There is no reason to believe that if affirmative action were eradicated in the near future, the deep, historical feelings that many members of the dominant culture have about blacks would dramatically change overnight. Thus, the price of nullifying affirmative action is far too high.

The majority of women interviewed believe that affirmative action will survive because corporations are aware that, for them to be competitive on the global market, a diverse workforce is absolutely necessary. These law professors also argued that a return to segregation would desolate the economic structure of our nation. Moreover, students benefit from being exposed to diverse faculty and viewpoints. There is pressure from corporations to continue programs of diversity and affirmative action programs in higher education. A few of the professors argue that as time progresses, the nation will witness support for affirmative action in places where you would not necessarily expect to find it, and they are confident such a sentiment will continue.[47] Judy Scales-Trent and Taunya Lovell Banks believed that affirmative action would take on different forms but will survive.[48]

Kimberly Jade Norwood believed that affirmative action policies that support legacies will continue. She argued that affirmative action designed to benefit minorities is under serious attack, and that supporters are losing the battle. She noted the significant inequalities in American society: "We know for a fact that black kids are arrested more, convicted more, sentenced more, sentenced longer. Blacks are put on death row more, actually executed more. Blacks continue to make less money for the same work, with identical resumes. . . . Yet every single time efforts are made to address these inequities, white America goes crazy and screams unfair!"[49] Beverly Moran was not optimistic. She believes that affirmative action is all but dead.[50]

Without affirmative action, many institutions of higher learning, including the legal academy, would have made little effort to ethnically diversify its faculties. In fact, many would probably prohibit people of color (and in some cases women) access to their institutions, no matter how politely or in no uncertain terms. Moreover, many would likely marginalize such faculty by relegating them to "ghettoized" positions, such as teaching courses on "minority" or "feminist-oriented" issues. Even with affirmative action as law today, a number of institutions still behave in such a manner.

Kimberlé Crenshaw, Dorothy Roberts, Kimberly Norwood, and Annette Gordon-Reed all believed that the challenge of the twenty-first century will be to acknowledge and address the fact that the legal academy, like all avenues of American society, is becoming ever more diverse. Further, it is imperative that considerable efforts be made to address diversity-related concerns, whether they come from blacks, Latinos, gays and lesbians, women, or other groups. They argued that a primary purpose of the legal academy is to represent individuals of all groups, and it is important that the effort to do so begin immediately through attentiveness to hiring efforts.[51] The future of the legal academy depends on it.

Notes

1. Stephanie M. Wildman, "Integration in the 1980s: The Dream of Diversity and the Cycle of Exclusion," *Tulane Law Review* 64 (1990): 1625.

2. Wildman, "Integration in the 1980s," 1625.

3. Wildman, "Integration in the 1980s," 1625.

4. Wildman and Grillo, *Privilege Revealed: How Invisible Preference Undermines America* (New York: New York University Press, 1996), 104.

5. Several of the law professors interviewed argued this fact.

6. Interview with Paulette Caldwell, March 26, 1997; interview with Taunya Lovell Banks, March 18, 1998; interview with Kimberle Crenshaw, March 11, 1999.

7. Every law professor interviewed discussed what they saw as significant effort to prohibit ethnic diversity by conservative factions in the legal academy.

8. The majority of law professors interviewed argued this point.

9. Wildman and Grillo, *Privilege Revealed*, 104.

10. Herma Hill Kay, "President's Message—Beyond Diversity: Accepting Differences," *Association of American Law Schools Newsletter*, April 1989, 1.

11. Kay, "President's Message," 6.

12. Interview with Anita Allen, February 24, 1997; Banks interview.

13. Wildman and Grillo, *Privilege Revealed*, 109.

14. Wildman and Grillo, *Privilege Revealed*, 109; Allen interview; Banks interview; Caldwell interview; Crenshaw interview.

15. Interview with Kimberly Jade Norwood, August 19, 2007; interview with Dorothy Roberts, September 20, 2007.

16. This was the consensus of the majority of women interviewed.

17. Every law professor that I interviewed echoed this sentiment.

18. Patricia J. Williams, *The Rooster's Egg: On the Persistence of Prejudice* (Cambridge, MA: Harvard University Press, 1995), 88.

19. Anita Hill, *Speaking Truth to Power* (New York: Doubleday, 1997), 46.

20. Interview with Anita Allen, February 27, 1997; Allen interview; Banks interview; Caldwell interview; Crenshaw interview; interview with Emma Coleman-Jordan, February 24, 1997; interview with Judy Scales-Trent, February 19, 1997.

21. Williams, *The Rooster's Egg*, 91.

22. Williams, *The Rooster's Egg*, 89.

23. Cheryl Harris, "Finding Sojourner's Truth: Race, Gender, and Institution of Property," *Cardozo Law Review* 18 (November 1996): 309–409.

24. Williams, *The Rooster's Egg*, 91–92.

25. Interview with Annette Gordon-Reed, January 5, 2001.

26. Gordon-Reed interview.

27. Williams, *The Rooster's Egg*, 92.

28. Allen interview.

29. Judy Scales-Trent, *Notes of a White, Black Woman: Race, Color, and Community* (University Park: Pennsylvania State University Press, 1995), 120.

30. Scales-Trent, *Notes of a White, Black Woman*, 120; Trent interview.

31. Williams, *The Rooster's Egg*, 105.

32. Williams, *The Rooster's Egg*, 105.

33. Interview with Lani Guinier, May 15, 1997.

34. Allen interview.

35. Guinier interview.

36. Interview with Dorothy Roberts, September 20, 2007.

37. Crenshaw interview.

38. *Shaw v. Reno*, 509 U.S. (1993); *Miller v. Johnson*, 515 U.S. (1995).

39. Crenshaw interview.

40. Interview with Joyce Hughes, June 26, 1997; Caldwell interview; Banks interview; Crenshaw interview.

41. Crenshaw interview.

42. Banks interview.

43. Wildman and Grillo, *Privilege Revealed*, 124–25.

44. These have been the major arguments or points of contention from a number of conservative organizations that have argued against affirmative action.

45. Elwood Watson, "Affirmative Action Still Needed in Our Society," *Delaware State News*, July 8, 1996.

46. All employment statistics have argued the fact that white women are the biggest beneficiaries of affirmative action.

47. Coleman-Jordan interview.

48. Scales-Trent interview; Banks interview.

49. Norwood interview.

50. Interview with Beverly Moran, September 5, 2007.

51. Crenshaw interview; Gordon-Reed interview; Norwood interview; Roberts interview.

CHAPTER FIVE

~

Interacting with Students: That Delicate Balance

Race, gender, ethnic background, sexual orientation, religion, and other categories are seen differently by different people. As the previous chapters have demonstrated, the sad reality is that cultural insensitivity, racism, and sexism are not strangers to the legal academy. Those groups who are newcomers to the academy find themselves fighting for respect, recognition, and a sense of fairness. In addition to faculty and administrators, there are other groups inside the legal academy that can be difficult to deal with. This dynamic is particularly true in the case of students. Such issues and stereotypes are prevalent.

Universities and the law schools within them are some of the few places where Americans have a real chance to participate in an integrated environment, one that is truly diverse in the broadest sense. Building a pluralistic community where individuals flourish regardless of race, color, creed, and sexual orientation is paramount in creating a progressive institution. With increasing resistance to affirmative action, tepid support for diverse work environments, and a hostility toward cultural pluralism in general, a number of institutions have been less than forceful in pushing for aggressive programs that advocate racial diversity. Despite such resistance, it is important to make this work visible, because it is a continuing process.[1] To quote one legal scholar, a white person can recede into privilege and not worry about racism whenever she or he chooses. People of color cannot. Men and heterosexuals can ignore the system of gender hierarchy, if they choose. Women and gay men cannot.[2]

As legal scholar Stephanie Wildman argued, "the authority privilege of the teacher crosscuts with other privilege systems in fascinating ways, because not all professors enter the classroom with the same package of privileges." According to Wildman, women concur that men are frequently given the benefit of the doubt, a little chip of "you belong here," whereas women usually are not granted such a courtesy.[3]

For black women in the legal academy, relationships with students can be a contentious, harrowing, and psychologically frustrating experience. Anita Hill says of her first-year teaching experience at the University of Oklahoma School of Law:

> My career progress at the university was rapid but not always easy. When I first arrived, there was considerable student unrest over faculty hiring. One matter in particular seemed to stir student resentment. The faculty had refused to hire a very popular white male professor in 1988, not too long after the period when I was hired. He and I did not teach the same subjects and were at considerably different levels of experience. In short, we were neither comparable nor in competition for the same job. Nevertheless, some students insisted on comparing us and argued that I had been unfairly hired over him.[4]

Throughout her tenure at the institution, Hill's competence was called into question.

Kimberlé Crenshaw strongly believes that the disempowerment and marginalization of women at various levels contribute to the challenge that black women law professors face in the classroom. Moreover, Crenshaw is convinced that women of color have an experience that is different from any other group. Women do not have maleness to fall back on as a way of establishing authority in the classroom. Moreover, black women in the legal academy do not have familiarity in the form of some kind of maternal figure to fall back on, whereas white women have been able to rely on white males at some level in this regard. Crenshaw described various challenges she had with students during her initial years in the classroom. White male students tended to be her biggest adversaries. White fraternity brothers (and in some cases, young black males) would challenge her intellect and make comments such as "Who are you?" or "What gives you the right to teach this class?" or "What right do you have to tell me anything?" They would always fail in their efforts to outsmart her, however.[5]

Anita Allen had similar experiences as well. Many of her students were not accustomed to having their performance judged by someone they did not see as their equal, someone they had never been taught to respect. Faced with such a dissonant experience, they sometimes lost all composure. They could not handle it.[6] Several of the law professors interviewed for this book found that some of these students coped better if they could reduce the role of the professor to a ministerial level, thinking, "It's just okay here and there, it's almost like an objective test, but there is no subjectivity involved in this." This arrangement is appealing to the majority of white students. However, when the professor's opinion or viewpoint is diametrically opposite to theirs, or if the professor dramatically defends her views, then these same, largely conservative students become upset. Because of this, black women law professors receive challenges in the classroom that others do not.[7]

Crenshaw stated that students would go to any length to see if you have come up short in any way. Students would ask questions just to see if you really are knowledgeable in your material. She also noted that although some students have no problem in challenging you, if you challenge them, they will interpret you as being difficult, combative, cold, hostile, or will have other female-related judgments about why you are being antagonistic, whereas male professors who challenge students are seen as having the right to be rigorous. White male teachers are seen as assertive, competent, and doing the students a favor for forcing them to rise to their potential. Yet when women professors (particularly women of color) force students to work to their full potential, they are seen as being unreasonable. Women are not supposed to require high standards. They are supposed to make things easy for you. Women should be nurturing and easy to work with. These are issues that are challenging.[8]

Crenshaw recounted a conversation that she had with one of her white female colleagues about what she saw as the double standard facing male and female faculty. Her colleague conceded that it was indeed a problem; however, she addressed the problem by appearing to be a big sister to the students. Crenshaw argued that while this response may be acceptable for a white woman, black women do not have such an option. If anything, Crenshaw argued, some of these white students probably perceived her as their maid or some other subservient role. But being able to appeal to a role of some degree of authority without being perceived as the father figure is available to many white women, and many take advantage of this in a range of professional contacts that are not available to people of color.

Crenshaw experienced the sexism that every woman experienced, but she argued that the ways in which white women are able to negotiate are sometimes racially closed to black women. Many men negotiate racism by making sure they establish authority in the classroom and are perceived as very good teachers. She mentioned the example of actor Sidney Poitier and his performance in the 1967 movie *To Sir with Love*. According to Crenshaw, Poitier, playing the role of a teacher, employed a black male strategy: "a little bit of toughness, a little bit of love, a lot of challenge." This approach, she argued, is off limits to black women law professors. It has been a real challenge for black women to negotiate both race and gender in an effort to feel useful and efficacious in the classroom.

Crenshaw argued that as a black law professor, she is privy to a lot of the interactions that take place between students (at least inside the classroom). Some students of color frequently drop by during office hours to discuss various issues with her. The dilemmas that African American and other students of color face in the legal academy are similar to the ones Crenshaw and her contemporaries faced as students in the 1970s and 1980s. Many African American students complain to her that when they speak up in class, they are often tuned out, that if the comment is one related to race or some other experience-related issue, white students are inclined to dismiss their comment as subjective or not particularly useful. Some white students put down their pens and stop taking notes when black students are speaking. Many white students assume that the majority of black students are in law school due to affirmative action preferences as opposed to merit. Because of this, there is a considerable amount of resistance toward students of color, who hear comments such as "My friend would be here if it were not for you."[9] These were the sorts of comments that Crenshaw heard during her years as a law student. Among law students, there is a large degree of self-selection about which students to study with, which students to invest in relationships with. This self-selection becomes part of an information stream, and the acculturation of black students in law school does not proceed at the same pace as the acculturation of a lot of white students.[10]

Crenshaw said that it took well into her second year as a law student at Harvard Law School to realize the significance of the *Harvard Law Review*. Relationships in law school are primarily reflective of the relationships that take place outside the academy. There are information networks that African Americans are marginally a part of, there are modes of acclimation to an institution that African Americans are often only remotely a part of, there are ranges of interactions between faculty and black students that are not a part of the larger university community. Any relationship that develops between a white faculty member and black student is more than often accidental and is an evolving one that takes place over the course of years, Crenshaw notes. She believed that the more experience white faculty have mentoring black students and other students of color, the more they will feel comfortable in doing so. According to Crenshaw, it is imperative for black students to recognize that they are in an environment that requires them to assume a different kind of stance than they are used to, and that this sort of conformity is not required of white students. It is the age-old question of the burdens of integration. Do people of color change to fit the institution, or does the institution change to accommodate those who are members of minority groups?

The problem for faculty and students of color is that they are not even aware of what the rules are and when they should be adjusting or not. Crenshaw did not believe that black students are inept at code switching, but rather, they have to be able to figure out the "rules" and then perform what allows you to push the buttons and receive the fruits that the academy has to offer for its victors. She argued that black law students and professors are for a time running a little behind everyone else because of code-switching, and that they are dealing with a set of institutional expectations that are communicated to them in convoluted ways.

Anita Allen described her experience in law school as atypical. The fact that she had already earned a PhD in philosophy before she entered law school embodied her with a sense of security. In fact, Allen said having that PhD made her "very cocky." She was able to be more casual about her experience in law school due to the fact that she would probably be able to use her alternative degree if she needed to. Also at this time, however, she developed an illness that caused her to become withdrawn and stifled her desire to compete. Her perception of the legal academy as a law student was that it was one of tremendous arrogance, elitism, and classism.[11]

In her first year of law school, Allen was told by a law professor that he did not direct his courses toward people like her, but rather, his goal was to persuade the white males who were going to law firms or to Wall Street to think more progressively about law. This professor viewed Allen, to use her term, as "being in the bag" and did not see it as worthwhile to invest his energies in someone who "had it made." This same professor would often rebuff her efforts to speak with him after class about various reading assignments and other student-related issues. Ironically, this professor considered himself very progressive. This experience forced Allen to become aware of the limitations of white liberalism. Moreover, the experience made Allen fully committed to being a supportive faculty mentor to black students as well as other students of color.

One advantage afforded black Generation X and Y law students (those born after 1965 and entering law schools in the late 1980s and afterward), according to Anita Allen and Kimberly Norwood, is that they have many more role models and much more opportunity for self-expression and excellence than Allen and Norwood's baby boomer cohorts did. However, both women argued that the downside is that this younger generation lacks the experience of history, of having gone through the most severe forms of discrimination. Allen argued that the younger generation tends to be more thin-skinned than some of the older generation who had to endure harsh injustices. Although

Allen says she was relatively impervious, she was nowhere near as tough as her predecessors, such as Patricia Harris, Sybil Dedmond Jones, Sadie Alexander, and others who learned to survive despite tremendous odds.[12]

Another issue of concern to Allen was the tendency of students in the mid-1990s to "self-segregate" by race, gender, sexual orientation, and other factors. Despite her criticism of such behavior, Allen understood how students could find some degree of solace by doing so, and she argues that in some cases, cultural identity can be a good thing. She quickly acknowledged how difficult it can be for young people to be left out of fraternity initiations or sorority rushes and left out of discussions in class, or to deal with other forms of exclusion or marginalization. Feelings of isolation aside, Allen made clear that it is unrealistic for black students, other students of color, or even white students to think that the larger society is going to operate in a similar manner, and they need to realize that fact, or they will be setting themselves up for all sorts of pitfalls. Over the past decade, Allen admits (as do some other professors) that there is considerably more interracial interaction among younger law students and students in general on college campuses.

Her viewpoints on multiculturalism echoed similar concerns. Allen believed that the phenomenon is a very welcomed development. In her undergraduate days, there was only one black faculty member to serve as a role model. There were no more than two black students per class, and there was no real effort toward or focus on any level of meaningful diversity. The same experience could be applied to her graduate school experience. Allen believed that multiculturalism has been a wonderful change, making student life richer, classroom life more intellectually rewarding, faculty affairs fairer, and scholarship more interesting.

Allen believed that minority students who are products of very strong public or ivy-league colleges can compete on equal terms with all white students and other minority ethnic students that they will encounter in law school. They are socialized already. Students who do not come out of such institutions or have had a more segregated prior experience tend to find that the transition from their previous life to law school can be bumpy. One summer, Allen taught a law school course for students who desired to attend law school but had not yet been admitted. She says a Latina law student approached her in tears. The student was distressed, fearing that she would have to give up speaking in the vernacular that she was accustomed to and acclimate herself to the linguistic jargon of the legal academy in an effort to be successful. The student was concerned that she would become isolated from her family, friends, and the larger community. Allen says the fear of "losing your culture" is prevalent among black students too.

Some black students voiced concerns to Allen that many white professors do not provide the sort of courses or employ the sort of materials that promote a meaningful level of diversity. Some minority students complained to her that the law school curriculum is overwhelmingly Eurocentric or does not focus on the sort of legal and social issues that are of concern to African Americans, and that their history is often out of the material. Another problem is the level of respect displayed in the classroom and how ideas are accepted in the classroom. According to Allen, some minority students said that professors did not call on them, or did not respond to their remarks as thoroughly as they did those of white students. Other minority students complained that they were only called on when the professor was looking for a black perspective or when the issues were about black people.

Some black students believed that it is more difficult for them to get white professors to provide them with substantial references for employment as law clerks or as lawyers. Allen believed the issue of faculty mentoring is a serious one. Some black students complained to her that they had a hard time finding a faculty mentor to work with in law school or to give the best of recommendations to them, or that they did not have an opportunity to receive the best clerkships and jobs.

Relationships between black faculty and students take on their own dynamics. Some black faculty see themselves as having a very important, central role and mentoring responsibilities. Others do not. In her early years as a law professor, Allen felt that black students in general did not call on black faculty very often for special attention; however, she was aware that some minority students frequently complained that other faculty of color could be distant and unavailable. Some of these problems can stem from class and ideological differences between students and faculty.

Taunya Lovell Banks believed that it is becoming much more difficult for black students who are the products of racially insular upbringings to successfully negotiate an integrated environment due to the fact that the insular community has changed so much as a result of integration. Banks said that in the segregated world she grew up in, she and her peers saw successful people who were lawyers, doctors, teachers, and other professionals. They also saw people from working-class backgrounds who were able to attend college. Banks argued that the inner cities now are plagued with retrograde elements that are detrimental to the inhabitants. The sort of parenting that was commonplace during the Jim Crow era has all but been replaced by children having children. Moreover, a sense of hopelessness has engulfed these environments as never before. This, according to Banks, makes the transition much harder than it was for those of her generation who made the transition in the 1960s. These are the students, according to Banks, that are most likely to drop out, have conflicts with both black and white students, and are seen as dysfunctional.[13]

Both Allen and Banks believed that the Hopwood decision of 1995 has had a slow but sure impact on minority enrollment in law schools. Both women have talked with many students of color who decided to forego law school or decided to enroll in law schools that were "diverse friendly." Banks believed that despite some levels of immaturity, many law students today are far more savvy than her generation and are not naïve to environments that appear to be hostile toward affirmative action or are not welcoming to people of color or women in general. To be sure, there will be those whose self-esteem has been defeated by the constant exposure to an unwelcoming environment, and they will have no confidence that they can survive and thrive in law school. This will be a major challenge for faculty of all races to combat.[14]

Annette Gordon-Reed argued that the relationship between black faculty and students is complicated by the huge demands placed on black faculty, particularly if you are untenured. You are supposed to be writing, serving on committees, and involved in other tasks. Writing takes time and energy. On the whole, during her time as a student, Gordon-Reed found her professors responsive, but very, very busy. She conceded that, as a professor, she has not always been as accessible as she should have been to students. She said that the publishing demands of her department limit the possibility of establishing meaningful relationships with students; however, she vowed that the goal of establishing a good rapport with students, particularly students of color, will be a primary goal for her.[15]

Gordon-Reed argued that due to the isolation that many black students face in the legal academy, it is important for black students to have accessibility to black professors. These students are trying to cope with law school and all of the tensions that such an environment creates. It is imperative for students and faculty to have a relationship because it is so beneficial. She noted that some of her colleagues have been successful in this regard.

Dorothy Roberts believed that despite recent attacks on affirmative action and other policies designed to promote inclusion, the state of black law students at present is fairly good. However, she and Emma Coleman-Jordan acknowledge that there are areas where racism and sexism perennially rear their head.[16]

Kimberly Jade Norwood, Dorothy Roberts, Anita Allen, and Kimberlé Crenshaw argued that many law students at their institutions long for an opportunity to interact with one another. However, all acknowledged that a certain degree of segregation and racism remains among some students. They noted racist graffiti, rumors circulating about African American students, questioning their intelligence and competence, and students being subjected to demeaning stereotypes. They say the myth that "you are only here because you are black" is commonplace at their institutions as well.[17] Several of these professors noted that black students often have to struggle to be seen as individuals. Some black students encounter feelings of isolation because others perceive them as tokens. Because they are so isolated, black students tend to gravitate toward one another. Consequently, this is seen by the larger community as an indication that these students are voluntarily segregating themselves. Moreover, considerable pressure is placed on black students and other students of color to conform to the norms set by white students. These professors viewed this as problematic, since many students of color have made a particular effort to associate with other students of color as a support system, needing such an environment for psychological and survival reasons.[18]

Judy Scales-Trent, Anita Allen, Joyce Hughes, and other professors made clear that African American students are not immune from being targets of some professors who feel that they are fair game. Many of these professors have their own personal prejudices and insecurities, and black students and other students of color tend to be convenient scapegoats. According to these women, white male professors are most likely to target students of color. Some of these faculty members have been abusive to students of color, and gay students as well. In institutions where the leadership is clear about the goals of the institution, these problems are less likely to occur. Faculty who are supportive of student diversity are rewarded, and those who resist it are not.[19]

Several of the professors said there has been an ambivalent relationship between black faculty and students. Black students bear the burden of criticism of black faculty by white students; thus, black students feel protective of black faculty. At the same time, these students do not want to be associated with the negative criticism that is frequently directed toward black faculty. As many of these women argued, a number of black students believe that black faculty should serve as mentors to black students, and that black faculty should be their protectors. To the extent that this does not happen, there is some degree of disappointment among black students. Despite such tension, in general, relationships between black faculty and students are more positive than negative.[20]

Lani Guinier believed that although people think and may even talk about race relations, for the most part, it is not a high priority for many people. Moreover, she argued, many students and some faculty fail to realize the level of polarization and inability to have a genuinely engaged experience across racial lines. She believed that for the most part, black students feel very alienated, besieged, and unappreciated. In contrast to Banks and Allen, Guinier believes that black students who are the products of historically black colleges and universities are more psychologically prepared for the complexities of the legal academy and thus perform better than black students from predominately white or mainstream institutions. The students from black colleges and universities are confident in their abilities and do not internalize the standards of the law school or use them as their yardstick.[21]

Guinier noted that when she was a student in law school, the climate was more conducive for student activism, and that black students and a few Latino students empowered her with a sense of community. Due to the dearth of Latino students, they aligned themselves with black students. There was a tremendous sense of community, of belonging, of social justice, a mission to change the institution, to change society at large, to mobilize. Such an environment, according to Guinier, was very positive in making students of color feel that they were connected, whereas now, students of all races tend to be more individualistic and career oriented. A number of the women law professors argued that the dynamics of race relations on campus have long-standing historical roots. Race and gender factors notwithstanding, people do not like to surrender power and hegemony and control. They feel threatened.

One law professor believed that minority enrollment in law schools will fluctuate but will not deviate to where it will threaten the white male power structure of the legal academy. She viewed the legal academy as an environment where people of diverse cultures are competing for a very slender piece of the pie. Because of this, the fighting becomes brutal. If you look at the 1960s and 1970s, she argued, at who was being counted in those numbers that reflected diversity, and compare those figures with the individuals who are supposed to be representative of the twenty-first century, it looks as if the numbers are increasing and we are getting a more diverse population, but in reality, the percentages of law students from certain ethnic minority groups are not increasing; they are decreasing.[22] The demographics are constantly changing.

Joyce Hughes described the relationships between white and black women at Northwestern University as strained and in many cases nonexistent. For several years during the early to mid 1990s, she and another white female law professor were asked to address the Women's Orientation group. Despite her status at the institution, some of the young white females had difficulty perceiving her as someone who could address their issues, and they always selected a white colleague of hers to be a dual speaker as well.

Hughes also mentioned a young black law student who was to meet with Hughes one afternoon to discuss a research project. The meeting time conflicted with a luncheon scheduled for the same date, and the student was adamant that Hughes reschedule their meeting so the student could attend the luncheon. Hughes granted the student's request, but five minutes after the luncheon began, the student returned to Hughes's office. When asked why she was not at the luncheon, the student responded, "Well, I went, but there was no reason for me to stay." She made no other comment. Hughes, however, had viewed the activity taking place at the luncheon, which was held in a courtyard she could see from her office. From what she witnessed, Hughes concluded that the white women there did not have it in them to embrace black women.[23]

Hughes noticed some similarities among black and Latino students, in that many of them came to law school with the intention that they were there for three years to earn their degree and graduate. Establishing relationships with other students is not a high priority for them. Part of this reasoning, according to Hughes, is that students of both groups are consistent victims of racism by a hostile white environment, and that distancing themselves from such resistance provides them with a coping mechanism. They will focus on their studies and succeed.

Concerning faculty relations with students, Hughes believed that many of her colleagues make a valiant attempt not to espouse any rhetoric that may be perceived as politically incorrect. However, sometimes inappropriate, insensitive comments are made. One student took issue with some comments that a professor made in regard to the O. J. Simpson trial. The professor made a comment about "how black people are" and said that black people did not know what they were doing in the O. J. Simpson case. In essence, the professor was disparaging black people. One black female student in the class was so distraught that she wanted to do something about it.

As another example of racial conflict, Hughes mentioned a multiracial student who challenged a viewpoint a white faculty member harbored. The faculty member did not like this, and he gave the student a poor grade. The student came to Hughes and discussed the situation with her. According to Hughes, the student was academically solid. Rather than mince words with the student, she told him that going toe-to-toe with a faculty member as a student, he would probably lose. Hughes believed that the faculty member, a vindictive person, was punishing the student for his positions. This same faculty member said that law faculty "should have minorities and women if they're up to standard." The professor probably did not even realize the racism that was prevalent in his comments.

A number of professors interviewed acknowledged that the make-up of the legal academy in the twenty-first century is considerably more diverse than when many of them were students in the 1970s and early 1980s. They stated that the number of Latino and Asian students has also increased. Lani Guinier believed that students and faculty of the current generation, generation x, and the millenials generation do not look at integration in the same manner today than when she was a student. She thought many people have either given up on the ideal or have decided that the goal is a vacuous one because there are clearly more important issues to combat.[24]

A number of professors interviewed believe that class is a factor in the legal academy and has become an issue of considerable importance to their fellow baby boomers. One professor argues that because of this, coupled with significant self-interest, there has been a concerted effort to secure power and privilege for like-minded friends and peers. The law students who presently populate the academy are much more likely to have enjoyed the benefits and efforts of baby boomers. This is certainly the case in regard to black students. It is less true of Latino students.[25]

This same professor believed that Latino students have not yet found their niche. Moreover, she believed that Latino students are reluctant to follow the path of blacks. Part of the reason for this reluctance is that institutions are more adept at challenging resistance from minority groups. She also argued that the Latino community is more fragmented. The fragmentations of the black community were smoothed over during the civil rights and black power movements. Generation X and the millennial generation are more diverse in general, and this in part explains the fragmentation among Latino students. Asian students have adopted an entirely different route. Such complexity could yield unexpected results, she believes.

Class prejudices and dynamics manifest themselves in various ways in the legal academy. This is in large part due to the emphasis that a number of white law faculty place on stigma. Judy Scales-Trent described a situation involving a Latino student that occurred during her first year as a professor. A number of her colleagues refused to mentor the student. The student had an impressive background: graduate degree, professional experience, board memberships. White students with similar backgrounds had been found acceptable. When Scales-Trent protested to one of her colleagues, he conceded that white faculty members preferred minority students who seemed "different," less confident, even though that was not fair. He also told her that it was important for her to start from the presumption that all white people are racists. Scales-Trent said she never forgot that lesson, that people of color will be punished for failing to behave in a manner that pacifies white superiority, for failing to act within the norms of what is expected of their ethnic group.[26]

Scales-Trent noted that whites are not the only people to engage in antagonistic, disrespectful behavior, and she described an experience she had with one black student: "it would be unfair not to say that other Black people try as hard as White people to take my yellow star away. They see themselves as tribal elders, able to grant or deny tribal membership at their whim. They will enroll me, or they won't. It must be intoxicating, exhilarating, to arrogate this power to exclude, especially if one has so little power to begin with. The Black student who received a poor grade in my course used his small power like a rapier. Frankly, I don't understand why you thought you hired a Black professor when you hired Professor Scales-Trent. She looks white to me."[27] Scales-Trent concluded that people of color can be their own worst enemies at times.

All of the women interviewed argue that, as law professors of color, they struggle with their status and position in the hierarchy that is legal education; however, they are aware that students struggle too. They believed that despite any differences, they have a special responsibility to provide black students and all students of color a feeling that they belong.

The struggle taking place in the academy to establish stronger relationships between students and faculty is part of this difficult struggle toward inclusive community. Despite attacks on affirmative action and smaller minority enrollments in some law schools, the fact remains that law school student bodies are more diverse than they have ever been. These results have primarily been fueled by aggressive students, deans, college presidents, and a number of law professors. Progressive members of the legal academy have recognized the relevance and importance of issues relating to race, gender, sexual orientation, and in some cases religion. They realize that addressing them is important in order for the legal academy to have any credibility as it prepares the next generation of students.[28]

Notes

1. Several of the law professors interviewed stated similar rhetoric.

2. Stephanie M. Wildman and Trina Grillo, *Privilege Revealed: How Invisible Preference Undermine America* (New York: New York University Press, 1997), 163.

3. Wildman and Grillo, *Privilege Revealed.*

4. Anita Hill, *Speaking Truth to Power* (New York: Doubleday, 1997), 87.

5. Interview with Kimberlé Crenshaw, March 11, 1999.

6. Interview with Anita Allen, February 24, 1997.

7. Allen interview; interview with Taunya Lovell Banks, March 18, 1998; Crenshaw interview.

8. Crenshaw interview.

9. Crenshaw interview.

10. Crenshaw interview. Several of the law professors interviewed expressed similar experiences.

11. Allen interview.

12. Allen interview; interview with Kimberly Jade Norwood, August 19, 2007.

13. Banks interview.

14. Allen interview; Banks interview.

15. Interview with Annette Gordon-Reed, January 5, 2001.

16. Interview with Dorothy Roberts, September 20, 2007; interview with Emma Coleman-Jordan, February 24, 1997.

17. Allen interview; Crenshaw interview; Norwood interview; Roberts interview.

18. Several professors interviewed echoed similar statements.

19. Allen interview; Hughes interview; interview with Judy Scales-Trent, February 19, 1997.

20. Allen interview; Coleman-Jordan interview; Crenshaw interview.

21. Interview with Lani Guinier, May 15, 1997.

22. This was the belief of one of the law professors interviewed.

23. Interview with Joyce Hughes, June 26, 1997.

24. Guinier interview.

25. This was the belief of one of the law professors interviewed.

26. Scales-Trent interview.

27. Judy Scales-Trent, *Notes of a White, Black Woman: Race, Color, Community* (University Park: Pennsylvania State University Press, 1995), 77.

28. This was the unanimous consensus of the professors interviewed.

~

CHAPTER SIX

Derrick Bell, Harvard Law School, and the Emergence of Black Feminist Jurisprudence

As we have witnessed in previous chapters, a large number of black women law professors have experienced isolation, marginalization, racism, sexism, elitism, and other injustices throughout various times in their careers. This prompted many of them to realize that they had many commonalities to discuss with one another. A few of these women decided to form a support group that would be academic as well as informal in an effort to address the issues that confronted all of them to some degree. One of the end results of the 1988 inaugural meeting of the Northeast Corridor Collective was the publication of the 1990–1991 *Berkeley Women's Law Journal* that discussed paternalism, sexism, racism, and other issues that confronted black women law professors.[1]

Moreover, a new form of legal scholarship known as black feminist jurisprudence evolved. Black feminist jurisprudence is an offspring of critical legal studies. Critical legal studies was a radical movement in mainly white male legal academic circles that originated in the late 1970s.[2] Initially, people of color, white women, and others were attracted to critical legal studies because it challenged conservative legal scholarship that was often racist and sexist in its treatment of women and minorities. However, as time progressed, many women and minority legal scholars believed that despite good intentions, many liberal white male legal scholars often excluded the perspectives of women and people of color and were not able to expand their perspectives beyond the worldview of progressive white male elites.[3]

The black feminist jurisprudence genre began to gain momentum in 1989. The genre developed because its proponents believed that the civil rights movement had stalled and the old 1950s and 1960s approaches of amicus briefs, marches, and litigation were outmoded in dealing with the more sophisticated racism of the late 1980s and early 1990s. Whereas some critical legal studies scholars seemed willing to abandon individual group rights, critical race theorists called for an expansion of such rights due to what they saw as the ineffectiveness of current laws.[4]

Members of the Northeast Corridor Collective, in which jurisprudence and critical race studies are represented, have produced hundreds of articles and numerous books. Through their writings, group members challenge racial orthodoxy and make its presence known in the legal academy. In addition, they question the ability of conventional legal strategies to deliver economic and social justice. Over the years, the group expanded its efforts to include issues such as hate speech, affirmative action, and critical white studies.[5] The catalytic event that prompted the Northeast Corridor Collective to take an active, public stance was the Derrick Bell incident that took place in the fall of 1989 at Harvard University.[6] Several of the professors interviewed weighed in on the Derrick Bell incident as well as the impact the incident had on them, the jurisprudence movement, and the legal academy in general.

In the fall of 1989, Derrick Bell, a tenured law professor at Harvard University, announced that he was going to take a leave of absence until the Harvard Law School appointed a woman of color to its faculty. The announcement of his protest made national headlines. The *New York Times* ran a series of articles on the incident.[7] The black female law professor who became the center of attention was Regina Austin, who currently teaches at the University of Pennsylvania School of Law. During the 1989–1990 academic year, Austin was a visiting professor at Harvard. Bell decided that he was going to champion the cause of Austin by putting pressure on Harvard to offer her a permanent position at the law school. Reaction was swift.

Immediately after he made his announcement, it appeared that everyone had an opinion about the incident—Derrick Bell, Harvard students, Harvard faculty, the legal community, media commentators, and many others. It seemed that the only person marginalized in the process was Austin. During the several weeks that the story remained in the news, Austin became the subject of scrutiny on many fronts. Her scholarship and credentials were called into question by some students, mainly conservative white male law students.[8]

Derrick Bell himself was not immune from criticism. While he received praise from a number of black people and some whites in certain quarters, there were critics, some of them black, who denounced his stance as grandstanding, showboating, paternalistic, and even sexist.[9] A number of people argued that Bell had no business challenging Harvard in such a manner. Others argued that his strident position would make it more difficult for a black woman professor to be admitted to the Harvard faculty.[10] After the tense and controversial year ended, Austin taught law at Stanford for a year and then became a faculty member at the University of Pennsylvania Law School. Bell left Harvard and is currently a professor of law at New York University School of Law. In the fall of 1998, Lani Guinier was the first African American woman to become a full member of the Harvard Law School faculty.

Joyce Hughes argued that Derrick Bell was acting true to the tradition of how progress has been made for African Americans. She quoted Frederick Douglass's powerful phrase: "Power concedes nothing without a demand." It was clear that the demand had to be made.[11] Speaking from her own experience as a pioneering law professor, Hughes made the case that history has demonstrated that something significant has to happen before radical change can occur. She states that there were black women who were qualified to be law professors before 1971, the date she became the first black woman on the faculty of the University of Minnesota.

Taunya Lovell Banks argued that the Derrick Bell controversy was instrumental to the feminist jurisprudence movement, in that after the controversy occurred, several black women from the Northeast Corridor Collective met at a colleague's home to discuss the incident. They were disgusted that such a movement was put into action without Regina Austin's knowledge, that it had been orchestrated without any consultation from any black women legal scholars. They felt that such behavior was sexist in its nature and was "business as usual," and they concluded that the interests of black men and women are often at odds with one another, and that black women's views and concerns are more than often marginalized.[12] These women were concerned that the Bell/Austin incident was seen as a race issue that was being led by a black man, and that black women were seen as the ever faithful choir girls being protected by their wise old black father.[13] Banks said that there was a considerable amount of resentment toward black men for not being more supportive.[14]

The women at this meeting made a valiant effort to talk about the situation in a constructive manner, due to the fact that Derrick Bell had been supportive to many of these women. They believed his intentions were in the right spirit, and furthermore, they were black women discussing a black man. There is a defensiveness, a sense of trying to protect black men.[15]

Taunya Lovell Banks credited fellow black law professor Emma Coleman-Jordan for being the brains behind the journal anthology that was devoted to the topic of black women law professors. According to Banks, none of the women thought that the anthology would have the impact that it had. Even today, the anthology stands as the only real work with a wide range of voices that represents the panorama of black women who are members of the legal academy. The commonalities and differences represented by these women are reflected in their essays. It is, in a sense, a lasting memorial of who these women are.[16]

Anita Allen, who accepted a visiting professor offer at Harvard the year following the Derrick Bell incident, was well aware that she was going to be greeted with intense scrutiny and would almost certainly not be offered a position by the law school. Allen noted that she knew Derrick Bell before the Harvard incident happened and in many ways viewed him as a father figure. She understood why Bell felt that he ought to make a dramatic statement on behalf of black women. He was accustomed to being their "father" of sorts. Allen argued, however, that Bell overlooked the fact that not all black women law professors had the same personal relationship with him. Regina Austin, for example, fell into a different category from Allen.[17] In fact, Bell conceded what he saw as his naïveté and unintentional sexism in regard to the Bell/Austin/Harvard controversy:

I was pleased that most Black women teaching law publicly supported my protest. There were some though—including some I had known for years and had encouraged and mentored—who reacted quite adversely to my protest. It was months before any of them spoke to me directly, but in the meantime I learned through others they resented the fact that I had announced my unpaid leave without first getting Austin's approval or at least giving her notice of my plans. They did not thank me for risking my own position to call national attention to the plight of Black female academics and criticized me for taking the public lead on the issue. As one of them put it, "None of us elected Bell as our leader and spokesperson."[18]

He further argued:

It is not difficult to find my failure to consider the effect of my protest on Regina Austin both selfish and sexist. Selfish in that the protestor's voluntary sacrifice of privacy, security, and the warmth of group identity carries with it the risk of involuntary sacrifice of those interests by loved ones and friends. As to sexism, I had conceded in my speech at the student rally that there was a patriarchal element in my protective feelings about the Black women students.

I viewed these women as both my students, to whom my greatest obligation was to teach by example, and surrogates for the daughters I never had.[19]

This controversy convinced Allen and the majority of her peers that it was time for black women legal scholars to find their voice. She stated that although Derrick Bell's behavior may have been seen as patronizing, it was in a roundabout way very useful. It forced black women for the first time to assert themselves as a group.[20]

Annette Gordon-Reed's reaction to the Bell controversy included gratitude for Professor Bell. She noted that he was well aware of the fact that it was black student activism that got him tenured at Harvard Law School, and because of this fact, he saw it as a way of demonstrating speaking truth to power. A group of people had helped him; therefore, it was his turn to help someone. Gordon-Reed acknowledged that there were those who felt that Bell was "too confrontational" in his approach; however, she argued that the stance he took was admirable in that it was a huge sacrifice for him. Gordon-Reed is convinced that it was Bell's individual activism that eventually led to the appointment of a tenured black female on the Harvard faculty (Lani Guinier), although Harvard would not admit it.[21]

Gordon-Reed believed that Harvard was probably under the impression that because it had five black men on the faculty, the issue of race was moot. She argued that Derrick Bell's protest was an extraordinary public example of support for black women in the legal academy. It was an issue of gender subsumed under the issue of race and how we make an effort to equalize these numbers.[22] Bell did make clear that he was filled with an unbridled passion about his position, and that nothing would have prohibited him from moving forward with what he saw as his pro-active agenda, regardless of what reservations Regina Austin or any of the other women, including his wife, Jewel, may have had. He commented on the event in retrospect:

> As for my failing to share my protest plans with Regina Austin, the women may have been right. At the time, though, consulting her seemed both unnecessary and unfair. Unnecessary because Austin seemed far more militant and insightful about whites and racism than I was. I found her writings invigorating and admired her outspoken statements on issues of race and gender. As to fairness, it seemed at the time an unfair burden to enlist Austin in my fight with Harvard. I had not consulted her before mounting a campaign that helped secure her visit. How could I approach her and ask whether she approved my putting my job on the line to support the student campaign to get minority women on the faculty? The permission would have been difficult for me to seek and her response even harder to follow had she said, "Don't do it." After all, I had already decided to go ahead despite my wife's reservations.[23]

Bell did have some degree of guilt about inadvertently thrusting Austin into a controversial spotlight. Moreover, he conceded that conflicting forces, such as unconscious sexism and a passion for justice, may have overwhelmed his pragmatism and led him to embrace the decision he did.[24]

Kimberlé Crenshaw was very sympathetic to Regina Austin. At the time, she was concerned that Austin would possibly become an accidental symbol of something that she did not have much agency in creating. It was difficult enough to be visiting at Harvard, let alone having yourself debated in the pages of the *New York Times*. You are talking about conditions that make it difficult for you to really settle in and be comfortable, which are conditions for being able to be efficacious and secure in your work. What could be more destructive, Crenshaw said, than to wake up and have your name discussed and not have that much of a role in such a decision?[25]

Crenshaw stated that she does not know if it was an unavoidable consequence of politicizing something, but it was an incident that could and should have been avoided. Sometimes, Crenshaw argued, many people are under the belief that change does not require breaking cement, or that you can get somewhere by just trying to slide into an institution. That is not what the critique is about. It is about recognizing that people should have some agency in their lives. She believed that while it is important to take an activist stance in struggles in all its contexts, it is also important that people be able to have some sense that a struggle is going on about them or around them or will involve them. It was Crenshaw's ultimate belief that the incident was not an affirming experience overall.

The reception that black feminist jurisprudence initially received in the legal academy was adequate, but like so many other areas of race- and gender-based scholarship, it was met with some degree of skepticism. Historically, Crenshaw argued, there has been the belief that jurisprudence is not grounded in any subjectivity, lacked any significant identity, and was basically objective, discursive engagement with abstract legal principles. Feminism largely challenged such a mindset on many fronts, she stated. It seemed like an animal that did not have any preexisting classification. It was clearly written from an engaging, interested perspective. It did not claim to be objective. It challenged what got constituted as objective. It was identity focused. It talked about power not as something external to the law, but that law simply mediated, that law constituted gender relationships.

Crenshaw argued that the ideals of feminist jurisprudence struck a lot of people as bizarre or gave them the perception that women were marginalizing themselves from critical discourse in the legal academy. They were either being sentimental or emotional, or were primarily concerned with cornering a "feminist" market for themselves. They could not see the larger picture. A large part of the project, Crenshaw said, was to justify and legitimize this kind of scholarship and to make the argument that a lot of the scholarship that preexisted was also self-referential, interested, and suggestive, but it masqueraded as objective under the guise of jurisprudence.

Black women legal scholars were not surprised by the "what is this stuff and why do we have it on our faculty?" reaction that greeted the dawn of feminist jurisprudence scholarship. Despite such initial opposition, several factors helped bring feminism to the table. A major asset was having white women who were major players in the field, Crenshaw said. During the late 1980s, the women's movement was still a visible presence on the American landscape. It was not at the heights that it had reached in the 1970s; however, it still embodied enough presence to have some influence, Crenshaw noted. It was still part of the general environment.

The relative visibility of the women's movement made it more legitimate to equate race and jurisprudence as one in which the law does not acknowledge difference, so the idea of talking and politicizing difference was not as controversial as the idea of talking about racial differences. Such an argument allowed you to get into the door. Afterward, you could fight about what difference differences made. There has been a slightly longer history of white women in law schools; as a result, black women were dealing with people who were a bit more closely aligned to those who really exercise power.[26]

A number of the early women law professors were wives, sisters, and daughters of men who were powerful people in the profession. This factor paved the way for an alternative manner of looking at the law. What was slightly more controversial was the sort of feminism that women of color introduced to the academy. This sort of jurisprudence was more than often of a rabidly different mindset and ended up being rhetoric that had to be defended in more stark terms.[27]

Kimberlé Crenshaw, like many of her legal cohorts, credited the networking opportunities that developed among black women legal scholars. She mentioned the late Denise Carty-Benia and fellow law professor Linda Greene during her final year as a law student at Harvard. Crenshaw argued that prior to having these two women as professors, she and other students of all races hardly knew that any black women law professors existed. She described Denise Carty-Benia in the classroom as a woman who appeared to be fearless, had a command of the language and the law that was just awe inspiring, and was still down with other black people. The black students could identify with her completely. The students, according to Crenshaw, were very endeared to her.[28]

Crenshaw realized retrospectively that she was not aware of how much pressure Carty-Benia had to bear, how many demands were placed on her by all kinds of people, and how emotionally and personally and professionally challenging it was to maintain a balance carrying all those entities forward. Moreover, she argued that the Northeast Corridor Collective was helpful in having black women legal scholars serve as a support network for one another. There was nothing more beneficial, Crenshaw states, than bringing like-minded, like-experienced women together to discuss issues that were important enough to be addressed collectively.

A number of black women law professors interviewed argued that in addition to providing crucial mentoring opportunities, the Northeast Corridor Collective meetings made it possible for them to discuss their scholarship with one another. Prior to the organization, a number of these law professors harbored feelings of isolation. They felt that they had no one with whom to discuss the sort of work they engaged in. The collective provided an environment where they could feel free to discuss their work.[29]

During my interview with her, Kimberlé Crenshaw discussed the findings of Claude Steele, a well-known black psychologist from Stanford University who had recently visited UCLA to discuss stereotype threat and how it shapes the performances of black students when they take a standardized test. She found professor Steele's talk interesting and believes that stereotypes affect the performance of everyone. Stereotypes shape how you feel about presenting your work to colleagues, recognizing that there is a possibility your work is going to be interpreted as substandard in some way, or problematic in its framing or in what you are trying to do. This is one of the major reasons that many scholars of color in the legal academy feel under the gun in terms of scholarship; in their experience, scholarship is onerous, a burden. So you need a community of people in which you can at least feel as though some of that tension is neutralized.[30]

Annette Gordon-Reed echoed similar sentiments. She stated that her case was somewhat odd, in that her primary work is in the field of history. There is something to be said for looking at other people's experiences and at comments that other, mainly nonblack scholars make about other people's work. The notion of writing from a black perspective, writing about black people, is new. Gordon-Reed believed that some critics, mainly whites but a small number of blacks, question such work as a viable scholarly enterprise. These individuals tend to be the sort of conservative scholars who question if anything even remotely connected to black studies is worthwhile, and they meet such studies with skepticism. Gordon-Reed believed that her history background has made her less vulnerable to attacks from critics of feminist jurisprudence. Moreover, she believed that historians, for the most part, are not all that deeply engaged in jurisprudence.[31]

Dorothy Roberts believed that black feminist jurisprudence has had a significant impact in the legal academy. She pointed to black feminists' concept of intersectionality, looking at how different identities and systems of power interact, and the methodology of storytelling from the perspective of scholarship. She is not certain what results black feminist jurisprudence has had on more traditional legal scholarship.[32] Kimberly Jade Norwood argued that black feminist jurisprudence has been extremely liberating; it provided black women the opportunity to read the stories of women who had undergone the identical situations that they had. She further argued that it is a form of literature that provides strength and determination for women of color and their allies. It is also a form of scholarship that is liberating and validating to progressive people of all races and both genders.[33]

A major belief among many black feminist jurisprudence scholars is that racism is an ordinary and fundamental part of American society, not an aberration that can be taken care of by legal means. A second belief among jurisprudence scholars is that people in power often manipulate events to promote their own self-interest. Out of this concern, many jurisprudence scholars decided to promote narrative racial theory.[34]

Narrative racial theory is a form of analysis that exposes the origins of racism and validates the experiences of people of color as being important by discussing their disenfranchisement in the legal system. Many jurisprudence scholars believe that white elites encourage racial progress for minorities as long as it promotes their white self-interest. As it has evolved, feminist jurisprudence has become a movement that harbors a healthy skepticism of traditional legal theories that support neutrality, the status quo, objectivity, color blindness, meritocracy, ahistoricism, and other largely conservative beliefs. Jurisprudence draws much of its philosophy from such intellectual traditions as Marxism, liberalism, feminism, law and society, postmodernism, pragmatism, and cultural nationalism.

Despite acknowledging the importance of having their support, some black feminist jurisprudence writers have occasionally had conflicts with their male critical race theory peers (of all races) and with white females. They have felt excluded by them.[35] The reason for such a feeling is that a number of black male critical race theorists view their experiences as identical to those of their black female cohorts. This often bothers many black women legal scholars, who argue that by irresponsibly promoting this point of identical experiences, black male legal scholars ignore the considerable impact that sexism has on their lives.[36]

Another argument of some black female jurisprudents is that much of the liberal and feminist jurisprudence scholarship that evolved since the late 1980s primarily discusses the experiences of white middle-class and upper-class women. In addition, it fails to realize that race is a critical variable in the life of men and women of color, and if the experiences of women of color are mentioned at all, it is minimal. A fundamental fact of jurisprudence is the important acknowledgment that women of color are distinctive from white women.

Much feminist legal theory prior to the late 1980s falsely assumed that the experiences of white, middle-class women represent all women. Legal scholar Angela Harris dispelled this assumption in her essay "Race and Essentialism in Feminist Legal Theory."[37] Like Harris, black female legal scholar Kathleen Neal Cleaver attacked mainstream white feminist monolithic ideology in her spellbinding article "Racism, Civil Rights, and Feminism."[38] Many black female law professors believe that their white colleagues perceive them as outsiders or primarily as tokens and role models for blacks and other minority students. Legal scholars have different interpretations of these labels. In her essay "Of Gentlemen and Role Models," Lani Guinier lauded the idea of having black female faculty serving as role models for black women law students.[39] But she preferred the term mentor rather than role model. She believed that the term role model diminishes the role that outsiders play, a role that benefits insiders as well as outsiders. However, Anita L. Allen, in her article "On Being a Role Model," was critical of the idea of promoting and hiring black women solely as role models. She argued that they must also be seen as competent scholars.[40]

Linda Greene, in "Tokens, Role Models, and Pedagogical Politics: Lamentations of an African-American Female Law Professor," referred to terms associated with tokenism: visibility, contrast, and assimilation. To Greene, these three terms imply that women of color are inferior and unsuitable to be law professors and should be challenged.[41] Legal scholar Jennifer Russell, in "On Being a Gorilla in Your Midst," made a similar argument.[42]

Other black law professors, like Taunya Lovell Banks, explored the differences between role models and mentors. Banks argued that the experiences of black women are unique and can enrich the legal academy.[43] Cheryl Harris, in "Law Professors of Color and the Academy: Of Poets and Kings," argued for black scholars in the legal academy to become agitators and to create a jurisprudence of resistance against the larger society.[44]

The conflicts that black women have with black men were addressed by Emma Coleman-Jordan in "Race, Gender, and Social Class in the Thomas

Sexual Harassment Hearings: The Hidden Fault Lines in Political Discourse." She argued that this was a case where race overshadowed gender and black women's issues were ignored. Moreover, she believed that the Thomas-Hill hearings represent age-old stereotypes of black women. In this case, black female law professor Anita Hill was depicted as delusional and untrustworthy.[45]

Issues of employment are also of concern for many feminist jurisprudence scholars. In her article "Sapphire Bound!" Regina Austin discussed the job termination of Crystal Chambers, a black unwed mother and single parent in Omaha, Nebraska. After she was fired, her vigorous court action was seen as symbolic of black women's tough and domineering nature. Austin called for black Americans to embrace Chambers and to see her as a positive role model for single motherhood.[46]

Paulette Caldwell, in "A Hairpiece: Perspectives on the Intersection of Race and Gender," discussed the case of Renee Rogers, a black female who was prohibited by her employer, American Airlines, from wearing her hair in braids. The legal analysis of the case was interwoven with Caldwell's story of being a law professor who wears her hair in braids. Moreover, Caldwell pointed out the inability of the law to provide a dual race-gender critique to uphold Rogers's right to wear her hair in the way she chose.[47]

In her book *Killing the Black Body*, Dorothy Roberts examined various examples in which the black female body has been maligned, marginalized, and disrespected.[48] In "Black Women and the Constitution: Finding Our Place, Asserting Our Rights," Judy Scales-Trent argued for a new legal interpretation by federal courts to revise the Fourteenth Amendment to include specific language that protects gender issues for black women. Scales-Trent argued that such a revision is needed because black women suffer from both racism and sexism.[49] Whether the issue is race or gender, the implementation of feminist jurisprudence in the legal writings of these women is now commonplace. It is clear that black feminist jurisprudence theory has made its mark as a viable area of scholarship in the legal academy.

A significant fact that distinguishes jurisprudence theorists from other legal scholars is that they are multidisciplinary: they draw on the works of men and women who are not legal scholars. This phenomenon has resulted in criticism by many scholars who engage in traditional legal scholarship. Moreover, jurisprudence scholars have been concerned with both the theory and practice of race and gender and have placed these disciplines at the center of their writings.[50]

Notes

1. "Black Women Law Professors: Building a Community at the Intersection of Race and Gender, A Symposium," *Berkeley Women's Law Journal* 6 (Winter–Spring 1990–1991).

2. Daniel Farber and Suzanna Sherry, *Beyond All Reason: The Radical Assault on Truth and American Law* (New York: Oxford University Press, 1998).

3. Adrien Wing, ed., *Critical Race Feminism: A Reader* (New York: New York University Press, 1997), 3.

4. Wing, *Critical Race Feminism*.

5. Wing, *Critical Race Feminism*.

6. Interview with Kimberlé Crenshaw, March 11, 1999.

7. Fox Butterfield, "Harvard Law School Torn by Race Issue," *New York Times*, April 25, 1990; "Old Rights Campaigner Leads a Harvard Battle," *New York Times*, May 21, 1990.

8. The *New York Times* ran a few stories on the comments of a small number of male students who were critical of professor Austin's pedagogy in the classroom.

9. A number of women interviewed for this book made it clear that while they believed Derrick Bell's gesture was sincere, they were also disturbed by what they felt was his paternalistic stance to addressing the issue of the dearth of black women law professors at Harvard.

10. Interview with Anita Allen, February 24, 1997.

11. Interview with Joyce Hughes, June 26, 1997.

12. Interview with Taunya Lovell Banks, March 18, 1998.

13. Banks interview; Allen interview.

14. Banks interview.

15. Allen interview; Banks interview; interview with Annette Gordon-Reed, January 5, 2001.

16. Banks interview.

17. Allen interview.

18. Derrick Bell, *Confronting Authority: Reflections of an Ardent Protestor* (New York: Beacon, 1994), 114.

19. Bell, *Confronting Authority*, 116.

20. Allen interview.

21. Gordon-Reed interview.

22. Gordon-Reed interview.

23. Bell, *Confronting Authority*, 114–15.

24. Bell, *Confronting Authority*.

25. Interview with Kimberlé Crenshaw, March 11, 1999.

26. Banks interview; Crenshaw interview.

27. Crenshaw interview.

28. Crenshaw interview.

29. Several of the law professors interviewed stated that the Northeast Corridor Collective was a major asset in both their careers and lives.

30. Crenshaw interview.

31. Gordon-Reed interview.

32. Interview with Dorothy Roberts, September 20, 2007.

33. Interview with Kimberly Jade Norwood, August 19, 2007.

34. Kimberlé Crenshaw, Cheryl Harris, and Adrien Wing are just some of the black women who are among the forerunners of this movement.

35. Crenshaw interview; Gordon-Reed interview.

36. This was a common complaint among several of the law professors interviewed.

37. Angela Harris, "Race and Essentialism in Feminist Legal Theory," *Stanford Law Review* 42 (1990): 581.

38. Kathleen Cleaver, "Racism, Civil Rights, and Feminism," *Critical Race Feminism: A Reader*, ed. Adrien Wing (New York: New York University Press, 1997), 35–43.

39. Lani Guinier, "Of Gentlemen and Role Models," *Berkeley Women's Law Journal* 6 (Winter–Spring 1990–1991): 93–106.

40. Anita Allen, "On Being a Role Model," *Berkeley Women's Law Review* 6 (Winter–Spring 1990–1991): 22–42.

41. Linda Greene, "Tokens, Role Models, and Pedagogical Politics: Lamentations of an African-American Female Law Professor," *Berkeley Women's Law Journal* 6 (Winter–Spring 1990–1991): 81–92.

42. Jennifer L. Russell, "On Being a Gorilla in Your Midst," *Harvard Civil Rights and Civil Liberties Law Review* 28 (Spring 1993): 259–62.

43. Taunya Lovell Banks, "Two Life Stories: Reflections of One Black Woman Law Professor," *Berkeley Women's Law Journal* 6 (Winter–Spring 1990–1991): 46–56.

44. Cheryl L. Harris, "Law Professors of Color and the Academy: Of Poets and Kings," *Chicago-Kent Law Review* 68 (Spring 1992): 331.

45. Emma Coleman-Jordan, "Race, Gender, and Social Class in the Thomas Sexual Harassment Hearings: The Hidden Fault Lines in Political Discourse," *Harvard Women's Law Journal* 15 (1992): 75–113.

46. Regina Austin, "Sapphire Bound!" *Wisconsin Law Review* 1 (1989): 539–78.

47. Paulette Caldwell, "A Hairpiece: Perspectives on the Intersection of Race and Gender," *Duke Law Journal* 163 (April 1991): 365–91.

48. Dorothy Roberts, *Killing the Black Body: Race, Reproduction, and the Meaning of Liberty* (New York: Random House, 1999).

49. Judy Scales-Trent, "Black Women and the Constitution: Finding Our Place, Asserting Our Rights," *Harvard Civil Rights and Civil Liberties Law Review* 24 (1989): 11–14.

50. Crenshaw interview.

CHAPTER SEVEN

~

Empowerment Within

Over the past two decades, women of all races have steadily entered careers in areas once considered exclusive male domains. Successes have been achieved in corporate America, the public sector, and academia. Yet despite the triumphs, the careers of women still lag behind those of men, especially in higher education.[1]

Although the number of women in the legal academy is increasing, racism and sexism remain serious problems. Women faculty and administrators often find themselves stagnating at the lower ranks and salaries. They also find themselves constantly faced with a white-male-dominated structure that seems impervious at times.[2] This ol' boy network exploits gender and race issues to create a glass ceiling. To succeed in the academy, African American female law faculty and administrators must not only learn the tricks of the trade but also become astute to the sophisticated and not so subtle nuances of the situations in which they find themselves. Moreover, they often are pressured to disavow all the characteristics that women are not supposed to display—aggressiveness, assertiveness, and dynamism, for example.[3] This personality transformation must come in the face of inevitable criticisms from male and female colleagues.[4] To quote one prominent black legal scholar:

> I was raised to be acutely conscious of the likelihood that, no matter what degree of professional or professor I became, people would greet and dismiss my femaleness as unreliable, untrustworthy, hostile, angry, powerless, irrational, and probably destitute.[5]

African American women have long sought advancement through the acquisition of an education. Historically, they have been denied equal access to secondary schools, colleges, and universities. This challenge continues for minority women. Since racism and sexism have been constant obstacles to their advancement in higher education, what is the future of African American women in the legal academy?

Each of the women interviewed had a distinct take on this question. Annette Gordon-Reed was optimistic; she believed that the forecast for black women aspiring to a career in the legal academy is bright. She argued that even since the 1980s, when she was in law school, many more women of all races are entering law school today with very strong academic credentials and are very capable people.[6]

The problem that black women will encounter, according to Gordon-Reed, is a more subtle version of "Jim and Jane Crow." She argued that there are still more than a few white males in the legal academy who harbor sexist and racist viewpoints, no matter how minimal, as to the ability of women to perform at the level of men, even if the woman in question has the credentials on paper. This mindset is particularly true toward women of color. As more older white males retire and are replaced by younger ones, and as more women acquire positions of power in the legal academy, Gordon-Reed believed that you will see the process really transform.

Gordon-Reed noted that colleagues such as Kimberlé Crenshaw, Anita Allen, Cheryl Harris, and others are fairly visible academics and are engaged in dynamic work. As a result, they are attracting young black people to the legal academy. One potential downside or barrier that Crenshaw perceived is that academia does not pay on par with other related professions.[7] Annette Gordon-Reed concurred and stated that it is difficult to create a pipeline to persuade students to become legal academics when they can work at a swanky law firm and become a millionaire.[8]

One professor found some merit in the idea that, absent subordination, discrimination, overtime, and similar factors, groups would be distributed occupationally pretty much according to their appearance in the population. She argued that from a social standpoint, the nation is in a predicament similar to the one it found itself in during the late nineteenth and early twentieth century. The *Plessy v. Ferguson*[9] decision and many other events in the mid to late 1890s set the tone for the early 1900s. Flash forward a century, this professor argues, and one can see the Supreme Court's jurisprudence since the 1980s as ushering in a new era of race relations for the next century. It is her belief that we are in for a rough time ideologically, but that the trend will result in an upward spiral.

According to this law professor, it is going to take a good deal of time and more reflection for women and people of color to figure out where they are and to decide where they and their respective groups want to arrive. Nonetheless, she was confident that the prognosis for black women in the legal academy is promising. Many younger faculty members have seen the positive changes that diversity has brought to the legal academy. Many of them are resistant to the judicial climate of the past decade. They resent being tarred with a broad brush of regression, racism, and class entrenchment that has come from some of the extreme elements of the political right. They are loath to return to the days of all-white classrooms. These professors believed that any lull in the number of people of color in the legal academy will be temporary.

Taunya Lovell Banks remarked that with the exception of Derrick Bell, Charles Lawrence, and Charles Ogletree, black women appear to be coming into more prominence than black men in the legal academy. This could be the result of a generational point where the legal academy has a critical mass of tenured women who are writing what they want to write at a time when older tenured men are at a later stage in their careers. In addition, many more women are prominent and active in legal associations than men. Over the past decade, there has been evidence that black women have a slightly higher rate of securing positions in the legal academy than previously. They are still overrepresented in the lower academic ranks, but the trend of hiring more women seems to have become the norm.[10]

Banks argued, however, that just because a person is hired does not automatically mean they will be granted tenure. The major concern for these women is how to earn tenure. A major concern of Banks was that many conservative law schools would revert to patterns that she witnessed in the 1970s: instead of having you go up for tenure review, the administration cuts you off at contract renewal time. Banks, along with other black women law professors, argued that there have been a number of examples where this has happened, both in the legal academy and in the larger academic community. Because of this trend, Banks believed we will see more black women in the legal academy who will play it safe, will be less outspoken, will write in traditional areas, and may harbor conservative positions on race.

Despite some feelings of disillusionment, Anita Allen had a positive outlook on the future for women of color in the legal academy. She saw some irony in the fact that during the late 1960s and early 1970s, it seemed that the world was coming around. She argued that it should not be all that surprising that the number of black female faculty is still relatively low. Patterns of world culture demonstrate that it takes a long time to undo the kinds of racism, sexism, and classism that have developed. Why should the legal academy be any different?[11]

Allen believed that one of the more positive developments in legal education has been the emergence of voice literature, a form of scholarship in which African American law professors have begun to talk about their experiences. Some baby boomers entering their sixties are able, for the first time in their lives, to discuss their work with passion. Allen noted the example of Emma Coleman-Jordan, who wrote an article on the topic of lynching that reflects some of her deepest fears and concerns about black America and its relations to white America.[12] Coleman-Jordan is representative of the generation of black women who entered the legal academy in the 1970s and 1980s and had to confront the result of centuries of degrading and negative stereotypes about people of color, particularly African Americans. These women have now gained the psychological and emotional strength to speak out. Allen further stated that the more recent generations of women of color law professors have not been saddled with such negative stereotypes and, because of this, will be much more comfortable tackling controversial issues that previously were off limits for discussion.[13] Dorothy Roberts believed that as more black women enter the legal academy, and as those who are senior take on more important roles as law deans, presidents of associations, and directors of centers, black women will have a greater influence on both scholarship and the culture of academia.[14]

Institutions of higher education have long been strongholds of segregation and employment discrimination. The legal academy is no exception. Although the number of women of color, including African Americans, has substantially increased in law schools, the numbers are not yet in proportion to the eligible population. Sexism in minority communities is as great a barrier to the academic advancement of women of color as is racism in the broader society; both must be eradicated to achieve a truly just society.[15] Limited progress has been made in faculty appointments and tenure for minority women, and minorities are still heavily concentrated in the lower ranks and hold a small percentage of administrative positions.

From 1900 until the middle 1960s, both the law student population in ABA/AALS schools and the legal profession in general were overwhelmingly white and male. Women lawyers of all races experienced difficulty in finding law firms willing to hire them. Sophia Mentschikoff, who became a partner at Spence, Hotchkiss, Parker, and Duryee in 1944, was one of the earliest of those few women who would become partners in Wall Street firms. In the 1950s and 1960s, other women could recount stories of their chilly reception from private law firms. Justice Sandra Day O'Connor, who graduated third in her class from Stanford Law School in 1953, remembered that the only law firm to offer her a job expected her to work as a legal secretary.[16]

Chief Justice Ellen Ash Peters of the Supreme Court of Connecticut began her career as a law professor at Yale in 1956 in part because she could not find a job in practice.[17] Judge Judith S. Kaye of the New York Court of Appeals pointed out that in the big Wall Street law firms, "enlightened recruiters in the 1950s and 1960s didn't bat an eye either turning away qualified women because the firm's quota of women was filled (meaning they had one) or offering a privileged few female invitees lower salaries than the men."[18]

By the mid-1960s, however, the demographics of the law school populations began to change dramatically. One reason was that virtually all law schools had removed the barriers that prevented the admission of women students.[19] Also, the civil rights movement and the reborn women's movement had stimulated women's interest in the legal profession. Many young women who were active participants in the civil rights movement in the early 1960s later turned their attention to studying law.[20]

The decade of the 1970s marked the beginning of a dramatic increase in the number of women law professors. In 1970, double-digit hiring arrived: fifteen women began teaching in ABA/AALS schools that year.[21] Two significant developments affecting law school policies helped ensure women would share in the general expansion of the legal profession. In the early 1970s, the AALS created a powerful new incentive for law schools to hire women law professors. At the annual meeting on December 30, 1970, the AALS became one of the first national academic organizations to prohibit sex discrimination in admissions, employment, and placement by its member schools.[22] In 1972, Congress extended Title VII of the Civil Rights Act of 1964, which prohibited employment based on race, gender, and several other factors, to university employment practices.[23]

By the early 1990s, there were 454 women chief executive officers in U.S. colleges and universities. Of that number, 7.5 percent were black and 85.6 percent were white. These accomplishments notwithstanding, race and gender segregation remains evident in higher education, from the faculty to the administrative level.[24]

As earlier mentioned, black women law professors face difficulty when it comes to tenure and promotion considerations. In addition to the overriding theme of racism, there is also the problem of the role that the black legal scholar is expected to play in institutions. At the majority of institutions, many demands are placed on these faculty members' time. Beyond classes, they are expected to serve on committees, work with student groups, provide service to the community, and conduct research. There is also the added obstacle of producing "acceptable" research and publishing in the "right" journals.[25]

Often, white institutions and scholars feel that they have cornered the epistemological market.[26] They tend to view research on race, gender, and ethnicity as not being legitimate scholarship, particularly when it is presented from an Afrocentric perspective, and they have the same perceptions of journals that publish this research. Since research is an important component of tenure and promotion considerations in all fields in higher education, such negative perceptions of African American feminist legal scholarship often place black women law professors at a stark disadvantage.[27]

Many mainstream white legal institutions tend to search for the African American legal scholar who is considered exceptional by all standards, setting a higher bar than that for white candidates.[28] Due to this fact, many very good scholars of color have no real chance of being hired. When black law professors are hired, they have often been expected to represent the black perspective or are frequently perceived to be experts in black issues. Many find themselves overburdened with being the minority representative on committees, the black spokesperson. They also suffer from social isolation.[29] Black women as well as black men will fit either easily or awkwardly into the isolating world of the Eurocentric legal academy, and many resign themselves to being the only black member of the faculty. Many more, however, find the experience less than rewarding.[30]

In all professions, minority women are the least well represented among tenured faculty. According to data in *Black Issues in Higher Education*, the number of African American women who were full-time faculty members in 1991 was 11,460. This number was minuscule when compared to the 143,049 white full-time female faculty members. Tenured black women faculty were negligible (6.6 percent) in comparison to white women tenured faculty (88.2 percent).[31] The numbers were not much better at the administrative level.

Women hold few chief executive positions in U.S. colleges and universities. In 1992, there were 454 women serving as presidents. Of these, 184 were in private four-year institutions, 164 in public four-year institutions, and 106 in two-year colleges. Of the 454, 85.6 percent were white and 7.5 percent were black.[32] The lowest percentage (8 percent) was in law. Of all minority administrators, 44 percent were women, and only 2 percent were deans.[33] In 2002, only 9.2 percent of black women law professors were deans, 4.1 percent were full professors, 14.5 percent associate professors, and 14.4 percent assistant professors.[34]

Black women law professors frequently have difficulty in gaining respect in the legal academy. They are often challenged by their nonblack colleagues and find it hard to exercise authority.[35] They argue that when men are assertive, they are regarded as exercising authority, whereas women who assert themselves are likely to be considered pushy. Thus there is a tendency on the part of men to emphasize gender in interactions with women.[36]

It is clear that the participation of black women in higher education in general is characterized by gender and racial disparities. As one black female academic stated, "In academia, the glass ceiling is a silent invisible barrier to one's upward mobility in the professional and administrative ranks."[37] African American women often find themselves in what is referred to as a "victim bind," which occurs when the institutional structures and political culture of the legal academy create and shape their career patterns and images. What are being created and reinforced are stereotypical perceptions, which are part and parcel of the institutional systems of race, gender, and power relations.[38] Coupled with the historical ramifications of slavery and patriarchy, these stereotypes have helped to reinforce the marginality of African American women.[39] Such situations are what law professor and legal scholar Pauli Murray referred to as "Jane and Jim Crow."[40]

With so many potential Pandora's boxes evident, the future of black women in the legal academy may appear to be dismal. Yet, more often than not, most black women law professors are optimistic. Many barriers remain, but they can be broken by collective efforts and commitments to diversify the legal academy.[41] On the occupational level, one needs to recognize the many problems confronting black women in the legal academy. These include difficulty with promotion and tenure, discrimination on the basis of race and sex, social isolation and marginalization, and the lack of rewards for professional activities. These problems hold true for black women professors in law schools.[42]

As has been stated previously, the paucity of black women law professors in faculty and administrative positions can be attributed to the few numbers in the doctoral pipeline. Until more black women enter graduate and professional programs and earn PhDs, MBAs, and law degrees, black representation in faculty and administrative posts will continue to be negligible. Beyond increasing and developing the talent pool, there are many other activities that will further enhance black women's leadership, such as mentoring and networking.[43] Tenure, promotions, and appointments to more substantive administrative posts will inevitably become the rule rather than the exception. Institutions must move beyond the tokenism that is so pervasive in the legal academy and in other areas of academia as well.[44]

Part of the responsibility of institutions is to validate black women's scholarship. Patricia Hill Collins eloquently argued the necessity of establishing a black feminist epistemology. She argued that since black women have been placed in marginal positions for so long, they must learn to become creative with their marginality—that is, they must use their "outsider within" status to create black feminist thought, an epistemology that reflects not only a special view of society but also a view of self and family. Armed with self-knowledge, black women are strengthened to break the glass ceiling.[45]

Mentoring is key to breaking the glass ceiling for black women. A survey conducted by Felicenne Ramey found that many black women cite having a mentor as key to their career development.[46] It is therefore critically important for administrative leaders to mentor young scholars who demonstrate the potential for assuming leadership positions. If the problem of too few African American women law faculty and administrators is to be rectified, a system of growing and developing future administrators and managers must become the responsibility of women who already have administrative skills and positions.[47] Tenured black law faculty must begin to help establish younger scholars and equip them for the long, arduous task of preparing for tenure.[48] Audre Lorde has argued that black women need to move beyond the occasional petty divisions that they have among themselves and work collectively toward increasing their visibility in all areas of life.[49]

More intensive career counseling is also needed for young black women to pursue careers in all areas of academia. Education experts Valara Washington and Joanne Newman pointed out that many black women do not enter institutions of higher education because they are pushed out of the educational system before they reach that level.[50] Dr. Nellie McKay reinforced this notion when she states that "to be Black and female in the academy has its own peculiar frustration because it was never intended for us to be here. . . . We are in spaces that have been appropriated for us."[51] Thus career counseling and nurturing need to occur at all levels of education, from kindergarten through graduate school.

The future of black women faculty in the legal academy lies in their learning to empower each other and to foster cooperation, thereby diminishing competition among their own ranks. Through mentoring and the formation of women's networks, the number of black women in higher education in general will continue to increase.[52] Black women law faculty must learn to surge forward and skillfully negotiate and conquer all potentially mitigating forces to become effective, successful, contributing members of the legal academy.[53] By achieving this, they will have made the legal academy an environment where scholars of color flourish.

Notes

1. Mamie E. Locke, "Striking the Delicate Balances: The Future of African American Women in the Academy," in *Black Women in the Academy: Promises and Perils*, ed. Lois Benjamin (Gainesville: University of Florida Press, 1997), 340.

2. Locke, "Striking the Delicate Balances."

3. Several of the law professors interviewed stated this as fact.

4. Locke, "Striking the Delicate Balances."

5. Patricia J. Williams, *The Alchemy of Race and Rights: Diary of a Law Professor* (Cambridge, MA: Harvard University Press, 1991).

6. Interview with Annette Gordon-Reed, January 5, 2001.

7. Interview with Kimberlé Crenshaw, March 11, 1999.

8. Gordon-Reed interview.

9. *Plessy v. Ferguson*, 163 U.S. (1896).

10. Interview with Taunya Lovell Banks, March 18, 1998.

11. Interview with Anita Allen, February 24, 1997.

12. Emma Coleman-Jordan, "Race, Gender, and Social Class in the Thomas Sexual Harassment Hearings: The Hidden Fault Lines of Political Discourse," in *Critical Race Feminism: A Reader*, ed. Adrien Katherine Wing (New York: New York University Press, 2003), 367–72.

13. Allen interview.

14. Interview with Dorothy Roberts, September 20, 2007.

15. Esmeralda Barnes, "The Black Female College Student: Striving to Make Her Mark," *Black Issues in Higher Education*, March 25, 1993, 30.

16. Laurence Bodine, "Sandra Day O'Connor," *ABA Journal* 69 (1983): 1394, 1396.

17. Interview with Ellen Ash Peters, Chief Justice Supreme Court of Connecticut, conducted by Herma Hill Kay, December 7, 1989.

18. Judith S. Kaye, "Women Lawyers in Big Firms: A Study in Progress toward Gender Equality," *Fordham Law Review* 47 (1988): 111, 112.

19. Harvard admitted women students in 1950. Robert Bocking Stevens, *Law School: Legal Education in America from the 1850s to the 1980s* (Chapel Hill: University of North Carolina Press, 1983), 83, citing U.S. Department of the Interior, Bureau of the Census, Women in Gainful Occupations, 1870–1970 (1979).

20. Peters interview by Kay.

21. Peters interview by Kay.

22. 1970 Proceedings of the Annual Meeting of the Association of American Law Schools, 126–60.

23. Civil Rights Act of 1964, Pub. L. 88-352, 702, 78 Stat. 255 (1964); Pub. L. 92-261, sec. 3, 702, 86 Stat. 103–4 (1972).

24. Jane C. Ollenburger and Helen A. Moore, *A Sociology of Women: The Intersection of Patriarchy, Capitalism, and Colonization* (Englewood Cliffs, NJ: Prentice-Hall, 1992), 22.

25. Interview with Joyce A. Hughes, June 26, 1997.

26. Locke, "Striking the Delicate Balances," 342.

27. Banks interview.

28. Allen interview.

29. Lois Benjamin, *The Black Elite: Facing the Color Line in the Twilight of the Twentieth Century* (Chicago: Nelson-Hall, 1991).

30. Interview with Judy Scales-Trent, February 19, 1997.

31. "Statistical Indicators for Academic Women," *Black Issues in Higher Education*, March 25, 1993, 28.

32. *Black Issues in Higher Education*, October 21, 1993, 24.

33. Judith G. Touchton and Lynne Davis, eds., *Fact Book on Women in Higher Education* (New York: Macmillan, 1991), 18.

34. Richard White, AALS Statistics from National Directory of Law Schools, 2001–2002.

35. A number of the black women law professors I interviewed stated this as fact.

36. Allen interview.

37. Mary Ann Williams, "The Ultimate Negotiation: Communication Challenges for African American Women in Higher Education," in *Perspectives on Minority Women in Higher Education*, ed. Lynne Brodie Welch (New York: Praeger, 1992), 93.

38. Gloria Jones Johnson, "The Victim-Bind Dilemma of Black Female Sociologists in Academe," *American Sociologist* 19 (Winter 1988): 312–22.

39. Paula Giddings, *When and Where I Enter: The Impact of Black Women on Race and Sex in America* (New York: William Morrow, 1984).

40. Pauli Murray, "The Liberation of Black Women," in *Voices of the New Feminism*, ed. Mary Lou Thompson (Boston: Beacon, 1970), 87–105.

41. Allen interview.

42. Hughes interview; Crenshaw interview.

43. Locke, "Striking the Delicate Balances," 344.

44. Banks interview; Scales-Trent interview.

45. Patricia Hill Collins, "Learning from the Outsider Within: The Sociological Significance of Black Feminist Thought," *Social Problems* 33 (October–December 1986): 14–32.

46. Felicenne Ramey, "Mentoring: Its Role in the Advancement of Women Administrators in Higher Education," *Black Issues in Higher Education*, October 21, 1993, 116.

47. Allen interview; Gordon-Reed interview; Roberts interview.

48. The overwhelming majority of black women law professors argued that mentoring was absolutely necessary for young black students to receive positive reinforcement from veterans in the legal academy.

49. Audre Lorde, "An Eye for an Eye," *Sister Outsider: Essays and Speeches* (Boston: Crossing, 1984).

50. Valora Washington and Joanna Newman, "Setting Our Own Agenda: Exploring the Meaning of Gender Disparities among Blacks in Higher Education," *Journal of Negro Education* 60 (1991): 19–35.

51. Quoted in Barnes, "The Black Female College Student," 24.

52. Every law professor interviewed believed that this situation will be the case.

53. This was the consensus among virtually every black women law professor I interviewed.

Index

1965 Voting Rights Act, 7

AALS (Association of American Law Schools), 50
AAUP (Association of American University Professors), 50
ABA (American Bar Association), 50
affirmative, action, 101
Afro-Saxon, 86
Alexander, Sadie, 114
Allen, Anita L., 8, 61, 78, 80, 86, 94, 99, 110, 113–18, 126–27, 132, 138–40
American Spectator, 25
Anita Hill-Clarence Thomas hearings, 75
Antioch Law School, 4, 5
Auerbach, Carl, 51
Austin, Regina, 8, 83, 124–28, 133, New York University School of Law, 125; Stanford, 125; University of Pennsylvania School of Law, 124

Baird, Zoe, 35
Bakke, Alan, 6
BALSA (Black American Law Students Association) 52–53

Banks, Taunya Lovell, 8, 14, 55, 57–59, 62, 83–86, 93, 97 103, 105, 115–16, 118, 125–26, 133, 139; Syracuse University, 86
Barry, Marion, 18
Bell, Derrick, 7, 124, 125, 126, 139
Bennett, William, 37
Berkeley Women's Law Journal, 2, 123
Biden, Joseph 14
Black feminist jurisprudence genre, 124, 131
Black Issues in Higher Education, 142
Bolick, Clint; *Wall Street Journal*, 36; NPR's *Morning Edition*, 36, 39, 41
Bonds, Barry, 18
Boortz, Neal, 25
Bork, Robert, 35; Supreme Court nominee, 42
Boxer, Barbara, 37
Bradley, Ed, 31
Brock, David, 24, 25; *Blinded by the Right: The Conscience of an Ex-Conservative*, 25
Brown v. Board of Education, 5, 78
Brown, Jim, 18

Cahn, Jean Camper, 4, 5
Caldwell, Paulette, 2, 83, 133
Carter, Stephen, 37, 40; *The Confirmation Mess: Cleaning Up the Federal Appointments Process*, 38; *The Tyranny of the Majority*, 37
Carty-Benia, Denise, 129, 130
Central Tennessee College, 49
Chambers, Crystal—Omaha, Nebraska, 133
Chavis, Benjamin, 18, 37
Chicago Tribune, 40
Civil Rights Act of 1964, 96
Civil Rights Act, 6
Civil Rights Division (of Attorney General's Office), 42
Cleaver, Kathleen Neal, 132
Clinton, Bill, 1, 2, 25, 34; Guinier nomination, 34, 35; *My Life*, in reference to Guinier Hearings, 41, 42
Coleman-Jordan, Emma, 7, 14, 116, 126, 133, 140
Collins, Patricia Hill, 143
Columbia Journalism Review, 37
Columbia University, 57, 98
Crenshaw, Kimberlé, 8, 14, 16, 25–28, 62, 74–75, 81–82, 102, 103, 105, 110–13, 116, 128–30, 138; Harvard Law School, 112; *Harvard Law Review*, 112; UCLA, 130
Critical legal studies, 80, 123
cultural nationalism, 131

Danforth, John, 28
Davis, Adrienne, 21, 22
Dedmond, Sybil Jones, 3, 4, 49, 114
DeFunis, March, 6
Democratic Party, 40
Designing Women, 22
Douglass, Frederick, 125

Elders, Jocelyn, 75
Equal Employment Opportunity Commission (EEOC), 14

Feinstein, Diane, 37
feminism, 131
Fischer, Mary A., 17
Fisk University, 87
Ford, Gerald, 37
Frontline, 19

Generation X and Y, 113
Generation X, 120
Gigot, Paul, 36
Glamour, 28
Gordon-Reed, Annette, 8, 13, 57, 80, 87, 105, 116, 127, 138
Greene, Linda, 129, 132
Grillo, Trina, 72, 73
Grover, Harry, 3
Guinier, Lani, 1, 2, 3, 13, 34–36, 38–42, 62, 76, 77, 117, 118, 120, 132; *Becoming Gentlemen*, 76; *Lift Every Voice*, 36; Harvard Law School faculty, 125; University of Pennsylvania School of Law, 34

Harris, Angela, 8, 72, 74, 132
Harris, Cheryl, 8, 98, 133, 138
Harris, Patricia Roberts, 4, 114
Harvard Law School, 7, 124, 127
Harvard University, 57, 124
Heflin, Howell, 19
Hill, Anita, 1, 2, 8, 13–17, 25, 29–34, 38, 42, 61, 96, 133; Clarence Thomas Supreme Court Hearings, 18–28; Yale Law School, 79; University of Oklahoma School of Law, 110; view on affirmative action, 96
hooks, bell, 30, 71
Hopwood decision of 1995, 116
Hopwood, Cheryl, 101
Hughes, Joyce Anne, 8, 49–55, 58, 83, 86, 117–19, 125

Imus, Don, 25
Iverson, Alan, 18

Jackson, Jesse, 18, 26
Jackson, Michael, 18
James, Rick, 18
Jim and Jane Crow, 138, 143
Jim Crow, 75, 115

Kay, Herma Hill, 94
Kaye, Judith S., 141
Kennedy, Edward, 37
King Jr., Martin Luther, 93

law and society, 131
Lawrence, Charles, 139
Leahy, Patrick, 37
liberalism, 131
Limbaugh, Rush, 25
Lockhard, William B., 54
Lorde, Audre, 144; *Sister Outsider*, 85
Los Angeles Times, 35
Lytle, Lutie A., 49

Marshall, Thurgood, 13
Marxism, 131
McCade, Jewel Jackson, 28
McKay, Nellie, 19, 144
Mentschikoff, Sophia, 140
Miller v. Johnson, 102
Minneapolis Star, 50
Minneapolis Urban League, 50, 53
Mississippi University for Women v. Hogan, 7
Monroe, Sylvester, 18
Moore, Hazel "Rasheeda," 18
Moran, Beverly, 8, 62–63, 85–86, 105
Mosley-Braun, Carol, 30, 37
Murphy, Eddie, 18
Murray, Pauli, 143

NAACP, 3, 37
Nabrit, Jr, James M., President of Howard University, 4
Narrative racial theory, 131
National Public Radio, 13
New York Times, 37, 124, 128

Newman, Joanne, 144
Newsday, 13
Newsweek, 35
North Carolina Central (law school), 49
North Carolina Central University School of Law, 3
Northeast Corridor Collective, 7, 8, 123–25, 130
Northwestern University School of Law, 83
Northwestern University, 79, 118
Norwood, Kimberly Jade, 6, 8, 61–63, 78, 81, 86, 95, 105, 113, 116, 131
NYU School of Law, 57

O. J. Simpson trial, 119
O'Connor, Justice Sandra Day, 7, 140; Stanford Law School, 141
Ogletree, Charles, 139
Oklahoma School of Law, 61

Painter, Nell Irvin, 17
Patrick, Deval, 42
Patterson, Orlando, 21
Peters, Ellen Ash, 141
Phi Beta Kappa, 87
Philadelphia Inquirer, 36
Plessy v. Ferguson, 138
Poitier, Sidney, 111
postmodernism, 131
pragmatism, 131

quota queen, 34

Ramey, Felicenne, 144
Reagan, Ronald, 42
Reed-Gordon, Annette, 98, 99
Roberts, Dorothy, 8, 63, 80, 85, 87, 95, 101, 103, 105, 116, 131, 140; *Killing the Black Body*, 133
Robinson, Mildred, 55
Russell, Jennifer, 132

Safire, William, 32
Savage, Gus, 18
Scales-Trent, Judy, 8, 61–62, 75, 77, 79, 80, 82, 99, 100, 105, 117, 120, 121, 133; *Notes of a White, Black Woman*, 60, 99; SUNY-Buffalo School of Law, 99
Scalia, Antonin, 31
Seidman, Ricki, 40
Shaw v. Reno, 102
Simpson, Alan, 36
Simpson, O. J., 18
Speaking Truth to Power, 14, 19, 28
Specter, Arlen, 19
Stanford, 57
Stansel, Mary, 18
Steele, Claude, 130
Supreme Court, 26

Texaco Case of 1997, 78
Thomas, Clarence, 1, 13, 16–18, 20–28, 31–35, 76
Thomas, Virginia, 24, 28
Thurmond, Strom, 28
Title VII of the 1964 Civil Rights Act, 78, 141
To Sir With Love, 111
Tyson, Mike, 18

U.S. News and World Report, 35
University of California at Davis, 6

University of Chicago, 64
University of Minnesota Law School, 49, 54
University of Oklahoma, 14
University of Texas Law School, 101
University of Washington Law School (Seattle), 6

Vanity Fair, 28
Village Voice, 39

Wall Street Journal, 41
Wall Street law firms, 113
Washington, Elsie, 18, 21, 29
Washington, Valara, 144
Whiffenpoofs, 80
White House, 40
Wiegand, Shirley, 19
Wilder, Doug, 34
Wildman, Stephanie, 21–22, 72–73, 93–94, 103, 110; *Privilege Revealed: How Invisible Preferences Undermine America*, 94
Will, George, 36
Williams, Juan, 18
Williams, Patricia, 8, 39, 79, 83, 86, 96, 99, 100; *The Rooster's Egg: On the Persistence of Prejudice*, 86, 98

Yale, 57
Yarborough, Marilyn, 55

~

About the Author

Elwood Watson is full professor of history and African American studies at East Tennessee State University. He is coeditor of two anthologies, *There She Is, Miss America: The Politics of Sex, Beauty and Race in America's Most Famous Pageant* and *The Oprah Phenomenon*. He is the sole editor of the anthology *Searching the Soul of Ally McBeal: Critical Essays*. His book *Outsiders Within: Black Women in the Legal Academy after Brown v. Board* was published in 2008 by Rowman & Littlefield. The author is coauthor of several award winning articles. His upcoming anthology is titled *Pimps, Wimps, Studs, Thugs and Gentlemen: Essays on Media Images of Masculinity* (Fall 2009). He is currently working on a forthcoming coedited anthology that examines the issue of anxiety as it relates to contemporary masculinity and a second book that explores the contemporary race realist movement.